Vue.js: Up and Running
Building Accessible and Performant Web Apps

Callum Macrae

Beijing · Boston · Farnham · Sebastopol · Tokyo

Vue.js: Up and Running

by Callum Macrae

Published by O'Reilly Media, Inc., 1005 Gravenstein Highway North, Sebastopol, CA 95472.

O'Reilly books may be purchased for educational, business, or sales promotional use. Online editions are also available for most titles (*http://oreilly.com/safari*). For more information, contact our corporate/institutional sales department: 800-998-9938 or *corporate@oreilly.com*.

Editors: Allyson MacDonald and Virginia Wilson	**Indexer:** Ellen Troutman-Zaig
Production Editor: Justin Billing	**Interior Designer:** David Futato
Copyeditor: Sharon Wilkey	**Cover Designer:** Karen Montgomery
Proofreader: Jasmine Kwityn	**Illustrator:** Rebecca Demarest

March 2018:   First Edition

Revision History for the First Edition

2018-02-23:   First Release

See *http://oreilly.com/catalog/errata.csp?isbn=9781491997246* for release details.

978-1-491-99724-6

[LSI]

Table of Contents

Preface

Frontend development is changing. Websites are becoming richer and more interactive, requiring us as frontend developers to add increasingly complicated functionality and use more powerful tools. It's easy enough to update a bit of text on a page by using jQuery, but as we need to do more—updating large, interactive sections of a page; handling complicated state; performing client-side routing; and simply writing and organizing a lot more code—using a JavaScript framework makes our jobs a lot easier.

A *framework* is a JavaScript tool that makes it easier for developers to create rich, interactive websites. Frameworks contain functionality that enable us to make a fully functional web application: manipulating complicated data and displaying it on the page, handling routing client-side instead of having to rely on a server, and sometimes even allowing us to create a full website that needs to hit the server only once for the initial download. *Vue.js* is the latest popular JavaScript framework and is rapidly increasing in popularity. Evan You, then working at Google, wrote and released the first version of Vue.js in early 2014. At the time of writing, it has over 75,000 stars on GitHub, making it the eighth most starred repository on GitHub, and that number is growing rapidly.[1] Vue has hundreds of collaborators and is downloaded from npm about 40,000 times every day. It contains features that are useful when developing websites and applications: a powerful templating syntax to write to the DOM and listen to events, reactivity so that you don't need to update the template after your data changes, and functionality that makes it easier for you to manipulate your data.

---

1 When I started writing this book, the repository had 65,000 stars on GitHub. It probably has many more than 75,000 by the time you read this!

Who This Book Is For

If you know HTML and JavaScript and are looking to take your knowledge to the next level by learning how to use a framework, this book is for you. You don't have to be amazing at JavaScript, but I don't explain what any of the JavaScript in the code examples is doing beyond the Vue.js functionality, so it's good to have some basic JavaScript knowledge. The code examples are also written using ECMAScript 2015, the latest version of JavaScript, and so contain language features such as const, fat-arrow functions, and destructuring. If you're not familiar with ES2015, don't worry—plenty of good articles and resources can help you with it,[2] and most of the code examples are pretty readable anyway.

If you're experienced with React, this book is still for you, but it might be worth checking out Appendix B, which explains some Vue.js concepts as compared to what you already know from React.

Book Layout

This book contains seven chapters and two appendixes:

Chapter 1, Vue.js: The Basics
> The first chapter introduces the basics of Vue.js, the main technology that this book is about. I explain how to install it and introduce it into a web page, and how you can use it to display data on a page.

Chapter 2, Components in Vue.js
> Vue.js allows—and encourages—you to split your code into components that you can then reuse around your codebase. This chapter explains exactly how you can do that to create a more maintainable and understandable codebase.

Chapter 3, Styling with Vue
> Every other section of the book deals with HTML and JavaScript, but this chapter presents the more visual side of creating websites. I explain how Vue works with CSS and styles in order to style your websites and applications, and the helper functionality it has built in to assist you with this.

Chapter 4, Render Functions and JSX
> In addition to the templating syntax that you'll recognize if you've seen much Vue code or read the Getting Started guide, Vue supports custom render functions, which also allow you to use JSX, a syntax you're familiar with if you've used React before. I explain how to use JSX in your Vue application in this chapter.

---

2 I recommend "Learn ES2016" on the Babel website (*https://babeljs.io/learn-es2015*).

Chapter 5, Client-Side Routing with vue-router

Vue by itself is just a view layer. To create an application with multiple pages that can be accessed without making a new request (or in buzzword format: a single-page application), you need to add vue-router to your website, which you can use to handle the routing—saying which code should be executed and displayed when a given path is requested. This chapter explains how to do just that.

Chapter 6, State Management with Vuex

In more complicated applications with many levels of components, passing data between components can become a bit of a pain. Vuex enables you to handle your application's state in one centralized place, and in this chapter I explain how you can use it to easily handle complicated application state.

Chapter 7, Testing Vue Components

By this point, you'll have learned everything you need to know to get your website running, but if you want to maintain your site in the future, you'll need to write tests for it. This chapter covers how to use vue-test-utils to write unit tests for your Vue components to ensure that they don't break in the future.

Appendix A, Bootstrapping Vue

vue-cli enables you to quickly bootstrap Vue applications from given templates. This short appendix shows you how it works and presents a few of the templates.

Appendix B, Vue from React

If you've used React before, you're probably familiar with a lot of the concepts of Vue. This appendix highlights some of the differences, and some of the similarities, between Vue and React.

Style Guide

The examples throughout this book follow the guidelines outlined in the official Vue Style Guide. Once you understand Vue and are looking to work on a larger app or collaborate with other people, I definitely recommend reading the style guide and following the guidelines.

You can find the style guide on the Vue.js website (*https://vuejs.org/*).

Conventions Used in This Book

The following typographical conventions are used in this book:

Italic

Indicates new terms, URLs, email addresses, filenames, and file extensions.

Constant width

    Used for program listings, as well as within paragraphs to refer to program elements such as variable or function names, databases, data types, environment variables, statements, and keywords.

Constant width bold

    Shows commands or other text that should be typed literally by the user.

Constant width italic

    Shows text that should be replaced with user-supplied values or by values determined by context.

    This element signifies a tip or suggestion.

    This element signifies a general note.

    This element indicates a warning or caution.

Using Code Examples

Supplemental material (code examples, exercises, etc.) is available for download at *https://resources.oreilly.com/examples/0636920103455*.

This book is here to help you get your job done. In general, if example code is offered with this book, you may use it in your programs and documentation. You do not need to contact us for permission unless you're reproducing a significant portion of the code. For example, writing a program that uses several chunks of code from this book does not require permission. Selling or distributing a CD-ROM of examples from O'Reilly books does require permission. Answering a question by citing this book and quoting example code does not require permission. Incorporating a significant amount of example code from this book into your product's documentation does require permission.

We appreciate, but do not require, attribution. An attribution usually includes the title, author, publisher, and ISBN. For example: "*Vue.js: Up and Running* by Callum Macrae (O'Reilly). Copyright 2018 Callum Macrae, 978-1-491-99724-6."

If you feel your use of code examples falls outside fair use or the permission given above, feel free to contact us at *permissions@oreilly.com*.

O'Reilly Safari

 *Safari* (formerly Safari Books Online) is a membership-based training and reference platform for enterprise, government, educators, and individuals.

Members have access to thousands of books, training videos, Learning Paths, interactive tutorials, and curated playlists from over 250 publishers, including O'Reilly Media, Harvard Business Review, Prentice Hall Professional, Addison-Wesley Professional, Microsoft Press, Sams, Que, Peachpit Press, Adobe, Focal Press, Cisco Press, John Wiley & Sons, Syngress, Morgan Kaufmann, IBM Redbooks, Packt, Adobe Press, FT Press, Apress, Manning, New Riders, McGraw-Hill, Jones & Bartlett, and Course Technology, among others.

For more information, please visit *http://oreilly.com/safari*.

How to Contact Us

Please address comments and questions concerning this book to the publisher:

> O'Reilly Media, Inc.
> 1005 Gravenstein Highway North
> Sebastopol, CA 95472
> 800-998-9938 (in the United States or Canada)
> 707-829-0515 (international or local)
> 707-829-0104 (fax)

We have a web page for this book, where we list errata, examples, and any additional information. You can access this page at *http://bit.ly/vuejsupandrunning*.

To comment or ask technical questions about this book, send email to *bookquestions@oreilly.com*.

For more information about our books, courses, conferences, and news, see our website at *http://www.oreilly.com*.

Find us on Facebook: *http://facebook.com/oreilly*

Follow us on Twitter: *http://twitter.com/oreillymedia*

Watch us on YouTube: *http://www.youtube.com/oreillymedia*

Acknowledgments

First off, an apology and a thank you to all my friends for putting up with me being a bit of a flake while writing this book. Now that I'm done writing, I will probably start speaking to you again.

Thanks especially to Michelle for being generally awesome and having good taste in music.

A big thank you to Juho Vepsäläinen and Rob Pemberton for helping me with the React examples. It's been a while since I wrote any React, so the help was appreciated! Thanks also to the other people I bounced ideas, sentences, and walls of text off while writing: Sab, Ash, Alex, Chris, Gaffen, and Dave, to name a few.

Thanks to everyone at O'Reilly Media who made this book possible, and thank you to the people—Chris Fritz, Jakub Juszczak, Kostas Maniatis, and Juan Vega—who provided technical feedback for this book that I learned a lot from.

CHAPTER 1

Vue.js: The Basics

As explained in the preface, *Vue.js* is the library at the heart of an ecosystem that allows us to create powerful client-side applications. We don't have to use the whole ecosystem just to build a website, though, so we'll start by looking at Vue by itself.

Why Vue.js?

Without a framework, we'd end up with a mess of unmaintainable code, the vast majority of which would be dealing with stuff that the framework abstracts away from us. Take the following two code examples, both of which download a list of items from an Ajax resource and display them on the page. The first one is powered by jQuery, while the second one is using Vue.

Using jQuery, we download the items, select the ul element, and then if there are items, we iterate through them, manually creating a list element, adding the is-blue class if wanted, and setting the text to be the item. Finally, we append it to the ul element:

```
<ul class="js-items"></ul>

<script>
  $(function () {
    $.get('https://example.com/items.json')
      .then(function (data) {
        var $itemsUl = $('.js-items');

        if (!data.items.length) {
          var $noItems = $('li');
          $noItems.text('Sorry, there are no items.');
          $itemsUl.append($noItems);
        } else {
          data.items.forEach(function (item) {
```

```
        var $newItem = $('li');
        $newItem.text(item);

        if (item.includes('blue')) {
          $newItem.addClass('is-blue');
        }

        $itemsUl.append($newItem);
      });
    }
  });
});
</script>
```

This is what the code does:

1. It makes an Ajax request using `$.get()`.

2. It selects the element matching `.js-items` and stores it in the `$itemsUl` object.

3. If there are no items in the list downloaded, it creates an `li` element, sets the text of the `li` element to indicate that there were no items, and adds it to the document.

   If there are items in the list, it iterates through them in a loop.

4. For every item in the list, it creates an `li` element and sets the text to be the item. Then, if the item contains the string `blue`, it sets the class of the element to `is-blue`. Finally, it adds the element to the document.

Every step had to be done manually—every element created and appended to the document individually. We have to read all the way through the code to work out exactly what is going on, and it isn't obvious at all at first glance.

With Vue, the code providing the same functionality is much simpler to read and understand—even if you're not yet familiar with Vue:

```
<ul class="js-items">
  <li v-if="!items.length">Sorry, there are no items.</li>
  <li v-for="item in items" :class="{ 'is-blue': item.includes('blue') }">
    {{ item }}</li>
</ul>
<script>
  new Vue({
    el: '.js-items',
    data: {
      items: []
    },
    created() {
      fetch('https://example.com/items.json')
        .then((res) => res.json())
        .then((data) => {
```

```
        this.items = data.items;
      });
  }
});
</script>
```

This code does the following:

1. It makes an Ajax request using `fetch()`.
2. It parses the response from JSON into a JavaScript object.
3. It stores the downloaded items in the `items` data property.

That's all the actual logic in the code. Now that the items have been downloaded and stored, we can use Vue's templating functionality to write the elements to the *Document Object Model* (DOM), which is how elements are represented on an HTML page. We tell Vue that we want one `li` element for every item and that the value should be `item`. Vue handles the creation of the elements and the setting of the class for us.

Don't worry about fully understanding the code example if you don't yet. I'll slow down and introduce the various concepts one at a time throughout the book.

Not only is the second example significantly shorter, but it's also a lot easier to read, as the actual logic of the app is completely separated from the view logic. Instead of having to wade through some jQuery to work out what is being added when, we can look at the template: if there are no items, a warning is displayed; otherwise, the items are displayed as list elements. The difference becomes even more noticeable with larger examples. Imagine we wanted to add a reload button to the page that would send a request to the server, get the new items, and update the page when the user clicks a button. With the Vue example, that's only a couple of additional lines of code, but with the jQuery example, things start to get complicated.

In addition to the core Vue framework, several libraries work great with Vue and are maintained by the same people who maintain Vue itself. For routing—displaying different content depending on the URL of the application—there's vue-router. For managing state—sharing data between components in one global store—there's vuex, and for unit testing Vue components, there's vue-test-utils. I cover all three of those libraries and give them a proper introduction later in the book: vue-router in Chapter 5, vuex in Chapter 6, and vue-test-utils in Chapter 7.

Installation and Setup

You don't need any special tools to install Vue. The following will do just fine:

```
<div id="app"></div>
```

```
<script src="https://unpkg.com/vue"></script>
<script>
  new Vue({
    el: '#app',
    created() {
      // This code will run on startup
    }
  });
</script>
```

This example contains three important things. First, there is a `div` with the ID `app`, which is where we're going to initiate Vue onto—for various reasons, we can't initiate it onto the body element itself. Then, we're downloading the CDN[1] version of Vue onto our page. You can also use a local copy of Vue, but for the sake of simplicity, we'll go with this for now. Finally, we're running some JavaScript of our own, which creates a new instance of `Vue` with the `el` property set pointing at the `div` previously mentioned.

That works great on simple pages, but with anything more complicated, you probably want to use a bundler such as webpack. Among other things, this will allow you to write your JavaScript using ECMAScript 2015 (and above), write one component per file and import components into other components, and write CSS scoped to a specific component (covered in more detail in Chapter 2).

vue-loader and webpack

vue-loader is a loader for webpack that allows you to write all the HTML, JavaScript, and CSS for a component in a single file. We'll be exploring it properly in Chapter 2, but for now all you need to know is how to install it. If you have an existing webpack setup or favorite webpack template, you can install it by installing vue-loader through npm, and then adding the following to your webpack loader configuration:

```
module: {
  loaders: [
    {
      test: /\.vue$/,
      loader: 'vue',
    },
    // ... your other loaders ...
  ]
}
```

---

1 A *content delivery network* (CDN) is hosted on someone else's servers all around the world for quick delivery. A CDN is useful for development and quick prototyping, but you should research whether it's right for you before using unpkg in production.

If you don't already have a webpack setup or you're struggling with adding vue-loader, don't worry! I've never managed to set up webpack from scratch either. There is a template you can use to set up a vue project using webpack that already has vue-loader installed. You can use it through vue-cli:

```
$ npm install --global vue-cli
$ vue init webpack
```

You'll then be asked a series of questions, such as what the project should be called and what dependencies it requires, and once you've answered them, vue-cli will set up a basic project for you:

```
❯ vue init webpack

? Generate project in current directory? Yes
? Project name vue-test
? Project description A Vue.js project
? Author Callum Macrae <callum@macr.ae>
? Vue build standalone
? Install vue-router? No
? Use ESLint to lint your code? No
? Setup unit tests with Karma + Mocha? No
? Setup e2e tests with Nightwatch? No

   vue-cli · Generated "vue-test".

   To get started:

     npm install
     npm run dev

   Documentation can be found at https://vuejs-templates.github.io/webpack
```

Try this now, and then follow the instruction it outputs to start the server.

Congratulations—you've just set up your first Vue project!

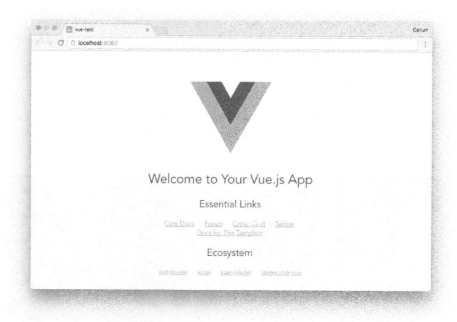

You can then explore the generated files to see what's going on. Most of the important stuff is happening in the *src* directory in the *.vue* files.

Templates, Data, and Directives

At the heart of Vue is a way to display data on the page. This is done using *templates*. Normal HTML is embellished using special attributes—known as *directives*—that we use to tell Vue what we want to happen and what it should do with the data we've provided it.

Let's jump straight into an example. The following example will display "Good morning!" in the morning, "Good afternoon!" until 6 p.m., and "Good evening!" after that:

```
<div id="app">
  <p v-if="isMorning">Good morning!</p>
  <p v-if="isAfternoon">Good afternoon!</p>
  <p v-if="isEvening">Good evening!</p>
</div>
<script>
  var hours = new Date().getHours();

  new Vue({
    el: '#app',
    data: {
      isMorning: hours < 12,
```

```
    isAfternoon: hours >= 12 && hours < 18,
    isEvening: hours >= 18
  }
 });
</script>
```

Let's talk about the last bit, first: the data object. This is how we tell Vue what data we want to display in the template. We've set three properties of the object—isMorning, isAfternoon, and isEvening—one of which is true, and two of which are false, depending what time of day it is.

Then, in the template, we're using the v-if directive to show only one of the three greetings, depending on what the variable is set to. The element that v-if is set on is displayed only if the value passed to it is truthy; otherwise, the element is not written to the page. If the time is 2:30 p.m., the following is output to the page:

```
<div id="app">
  <p>Good afternoon!</p>
</div>
```

 Although Vue has reactive functionality, the preceding example is not reactive, and the page will not update when the time changes. We'll cover reactivity in more detail later.

Quite a bit of duplication occurs in the previous example, though: it would be better if we could set the time as a data variable and then do the comparison logic in the template. Luckily, we can! Vue evaluates simple expressions inside v-if:

```
<div id="app">
  <p v-if="hours < 12">Good morning!</p>
  <p v-if="hours >= 12 && hours < 18">Good afternoon!</p>
  <p v-if="hours >= 18">Good evening!</p>
</div>
<script>
  new Vue({
    el: '#app',
    data: {
      hours: new Date().getHours()
    }
  });
</script>
```

Writing code in this manner, with the business logic in the JavaScript and the view logic in the template, means that we can tell at a glance exactly what will be displayed when on the page. This is a much better approach than having the code responsible for deciding whether to show or hide the element in some JavaScript far away from the element in question.

Later, we'll be looking at computed properties, which we can use to make the preceding code a lot cleaner—it's a bit repetitive.

In addition to using directives, we can also pass data into templates by using interpolation, as follows:

```
<div id="app">
  <p>Hello, {{ greetee }}!</p>
</div>
<script>
  new Vue({
    el: '#app',
    data: {
      greetee: 'world'
    }
  });
</script>
```

This outputs the following to the page:

```
<div id="app">
  <p>Hello, world!</p>
</div>
```

We can also combine the two, using both directives and interpolation to show some text only if it is defined or useful. See if you can figure out what the following code displays on the page and when:

```
<div id="app">
  <p v-if="path === '/'">You are on the home page</p>
  <p v-else>You're on {{ path }}</p>
</div>
<script>
  new Vue({
    el: '#app',
    data: {
      path: location.pathname
    }
  });
</script>
```

`location.pathname` is the path in the URL of the page, so it can be "/" when on the root of the site, or "/post/1635" when somewhere else on the site. The preceding code tells you whether you're on the home page of the site: in a `v-if` directive, it tests whether the path is equal to "/" (and the user is therefore on the root page of the site), and then we're introduced to a new directive, `v-else`. It's pretty simple: when used after an element with `v-if`, it works like the `else` statement of an if-else statement. The second element is displayed on the page only when the first element is not.

In addition to being able to pass through strings and numbers, as you've seen, it's also possible to pass other types of data into templates. Because we can execute simple expressions in the templates, we can pass an array or object into the template and look up a single property or item:

```
<div id="app">
  <p>The second dog is {{ dogs[1] }}</p>
  <p>All the dogs are {{ dogs }}</p>
</div>
<script>
  new Vue({
    el: '#app',
    data: {
      dogs: ['Rex', 'Rover', 'Henrietta', 'Alan']
    }
  });
</script>
```

The following is output to the page:

```
The second dog is Rover

All the dogs are [ "Rex", "Rover", "henrietta", "Alan" ]
```

As you can see, if you output a whole array or object to the page, Vue outputs the JSON-encoded value to the page. This can be useful when debugging instead of logging to console, as the value displayed on the page will update whenever the value changes.

v-if Versus v-show

You met v-if in the previous section to show and hide an element, but how does it do that, and what's the difference between it and the similar sounding v-show?

If the value of a v-if directive evaluates to falsy,[2] the element isn't output to the DOM.

The following Vue template

```
<div v-if="true">one</div>
<div v-if="false">two</div>
```

results in the following output:

```
<div>one</div>
```

Compare that to v-show, which uses CSS to show and hide the element.

---

2 A *falsy* value is a value that is false, undefined, null, 0, "", or NaN.

The following Vue template

```
<div v-show="true">one</div>
<div v-show="false">two</div>
```

results in the following output:

```
<div>one</div>
<div style="display: none">one</div>
```

Your users will (probably) see the same thing, but other implications and differences exist between the two.

First, because the inside element hidden using v-if isn't going to be displayed, Vue doesn't try to generate the HTML; this isn't the case with the v-show example. This means that v-if is better for hiding stuff that hasn't loaded yet.

In this example, an error will be thrown:

```
<div id="app">
  <div v-show="user">
    <p>User name: {{ user.name }}</p>
  </div>
</div>

<script>
  new Vue({
    el: '#app',
    data: {
      user: undefined
    }
  });
</script>
```

The reason the error will be thrown is that Vue has attempted to execute user.name—a property of an object that doesn't exist. The same example using v-if works just fine, because Vue doesn't attempt to generate the inside of the element until the v-if statement is truthy.

Also, two conditionals are related to v-if: v-else-if and v-else. They behave pretty much as you'd expect:

```
<div v-if="state === 'loading'">Loading...</div>
<div v-else-if="state === 'error'">An error occurred</div>
<div v-else>...our content!</div>
```

The first div displays if state is loading, the second if state is error, and the third if state is anything else. Only one of the elements will display at a time.

OK, so having seen that, why would anyone want to use v-show?

Using v-if has a performance cost. Every time an element is added or removed, work has to be done to generate the DOM tree underneath it, which can sometimes be a lot of stuff. v-show has no such cost beyond the initial setup cost. If you're expecting something to change frequently, v-show might be the best choice.

Also, if the element contains any images, then hiding the parent with only CSS allows the browser to download the image ahead of it being displayed, meaning that it can be displayed as soon as v-show becomes truthy. Otherwise, it wouldn't start downloading until it was supposed to be displayed.

Looping in Templates

Another directive I find myself using a lot is the v-for directive, which loops through the elements of an array or object, outputting the element multiple times. Take the following example:

```
<div id="app">
  <ul>
    <li v-for="dog in dogs">{{ dog }}</li>
  </ul>
</div>
<script>
  new Vue({
    el: '#app',
    data: {
      dogs: ['Rex', 'Rover', 'Henrietta', 'Alan']
    }
  });
</script>
```

That outputs every item of the array to the page in list elements, like this:

```
<div id="app">
  <ul>
    <li>Rex</li>
    <li>Rover</li>
    <li>Henrietta</li>
    <li>Alan</li>
  </ul>
</div>
```

The v-for directive also works with objects. Consider the following example, which takes an object containing the average rent of a few cities and outputs them to the page:

```
<div id="app">
  <ul>
    <li v-for="(rent, city) in averageRent">
      The average rent in {{ city }} is ${{ rent }}</li>
  </ul>
</div>
<script>
  new Vue({
```

```
      el: '#app',
      data: {
        averageRent: {
          london: 1650,
          paris: 1730,
          NYC: 3680
        }
      }
    });
  </script>
```

The syntax here is slightly different, because we want to get the key as well—having just the rent on the page but not the names of cities wouldn't be too useful. However, if we don't want the keys, we can use the same syntax as before, v-for="rent in averageRent". This also applies to arrays: if we want the index of an array, we can use the bracket and comma syntax that you just saw with the array: v-for="(dog, i) in dogs".

Note the order of the arguments: it's (value, key), not the other way around.

Finally, if you just want a simple counter, you can pass a number in as the argument. The following outputs the numbers 1 to 10:

```
<div id="app">
  <ul>
    <li v-for="n in 10">{{ n }}</li>
  </ul>
</div>
<script>
  new Vue({
    el: '#app'
  });
</script>
```

You might have expected the numbers 0 to 9 to be output, but that isn't the case. To start the list at 0, it's usually easier to refer to n - 1 instead of just n.

Binding Arguments

Some directives, such as v-bind, take arguments. The v-bind directive is used to bind a value to an HTML attribute. For instance, the following example binds the value submit to the button type:

```
<div id="app">
  <button v-bind:type="buttonType">Test button</button>
</div>
<script>
  new Vue({
    el: '#app',
    data: {
```

```
      buttonType: 'submit'
    }
  });
</script>
```

The following is output to the document:

```
<button type="submit">Test button</button>
```

v-bind is the name of the directive, and type is the argument: in this case, the name of the attribute we want to bind the given variable to. buttonType is the value.

This also works with properties, such as disabled and checked: if the expression passed is truthy, the output element will have the property, and if it is falsy, the element will not:

```
<div id="app">
  <button v-bind:disabled="buttonDisabled">Test button</button>
</div>
<script>
  new Vue({
    el: '#app',
    data: {
      buttonDisabled: true
    }
  });
</script>
```

When using v-bind with a lot of attributes, it can be pretty repetitive to write it out multiple times. There's a shorter way to write it: you can omit the v-bind part of the directive and use a colon. For example, this is how you would rewrite the preceding code example using the shorter syntax:

```
<div id="app">
  <button :disabled="buttonDisabled">Test button</button>
</div>
<script>
  new Vue({
    el: '#app',
    data: {
      buttonDisabled: true
    }
  });
</script>
```

While your choice of syntax is obviously a personal preference, I much prefer the shorter syntax and rarely write v-bind in my code.

Whether you choose to use v-bind or the shorter syntax, try to keep it consistent. Using v-bind in some places and the shorter syntax in others can get a bit confusing.

Reactivity

The last few sections of this chapter have shown how we can use Vue to output HTML to the DOM from values in JavaScript—but so what? What makes Vue different from any templating language?

In addition to creating the HTML in the first place, Vue watches the data object for changes and updates the DOM when the data changes. To demonstrate this, let's make a simple timer app that tells you how long the page has been open. We'll need only one variable, which we'll call seconds, and we'll use setInterval to increment that variable once a second:

```
<div id="app">
  <p>{{ seconds }} seconds have elapsed since you opened the page.</p>
</div>
<script>
  new Vue({
    el: '#app',
    data: {
      seconds: 0
    },
    created() {
      setInterval(() => {
        this.seconds++;
      }, 1000);
    }
  });
</script>
```

The create function runs when the app is initiated. We'll cover the Vue life-cycle hooks in more detail later, so don't worry about the function too much for now. this.seconds in that function refers directly to the value in the data object, and manipulating it updates the template.

Here's that example after the page has been open for a bit:

```
14 seconds have elapsed since you opened the page.
```

In addition to working with interpolation to output the value to the page, Vue's reactivity functionality also works when using a property of the data object as an attribute to a directive. For example, if in the v-bind example we ran this.buttonDisabled = !this.buttonDisabled; once a second, we would see that the button disabled property would be toggled once a second: the button would be enabled for a second, and then disabled for another.

Reactivity is an extremely important feature and part of what makes Vue so powerful. You'll be seeing it a lot both in this book and in any Vue projects you work on.

How It Works

This section is a bit more advanced; feel free to skip it and come back to it later if you don't understand everything.

Vue's reactivity works by modifying every object added to the data object so that Vue is notified when it changes. Every property in an object is replaced with a getter and setter so that you can use the object as a normal object, but when you change the property, Vue knows that it has changed.

Take the following object:

```
const data = {
  userId: 10
};
```

When `userId` is changed, how do you know it has been changed? You could store a copy of the object and compare them to each other, but that's not the most efficient way of doing it. That's called *dirty checking*, and it's the way Angular 1 did it.

Instead, you can override the property by using `Object.defineProperty()`:

```
const storedData = {};

storedData.userId = data.userId;

Object.defineProperty(data, 'userId', {
  get() {
    return storedData.userId;
  },
  set(value) {
    console.log('User ID changed!');
    storedData.userId = value;
  },
  configurable: true,
  enumerable: true
};
```

This isn't exactly how Vue does it, but it's a good way to think about it.

Vue also wraps some array methods such as `.splice()` on observed arrays with a proxy method to observe when the method is called. This is so that when you call `.splice()`, Vue knows that you've updated the array, and any necessary view updates can be triggered.

For more information on how reactivity works in Vue, check out the "Reactivity in Depth" section of the official documentation (*http://bit.ly/2sLXswZ*).

Caveats

There are some limitations to how this works. Understanding how Vue's reactivity works can help you know the caveats, or you could just memorize the list. Only a few caveats exist, so it's not too tricky to memorize them.

Adding new properties to an object

Because the getter/setter functions are added when the instance is initialized, only existing properties are reactive; when you add a new property, it won't be reactive if you do it directly:

```
const vm = new Vue({
  data: {
    formData: {
      username: 'someuser'
    }
  }
});

vm.formData.name = 'Some User';
```

While the `formData.username` property will be reactive and respond to changes, the `formData.name` property will not. There are a few ways around this.

The easiest way is to define the property on the object on initialization, but with a value of `undefined`. The `formData` object in the previous example would become this:

```
formData: {
  username: 'someuser',
  name: undefined
}
```

Alternatively—and this is most useful if you're updating multiple properties at the same time—you can use `Object.assign()` to create a new object and override the only object:

```
vm.formData = Object.assign({}, vm.formData, {
  name: 'Some User'
});
```

Finally, Vue provides a function called `Vue.set()` that you can use to set reactive properties:

```
Vue.set(vm.formData, 'name', 'Some User');
```

When inside a component, this function is also available as `this.$set`.

Setting items on an array

You can't directly set items on an array by using the index. The following will not work:

```
const vm = new Vue({
  data: {
    dogs: ['Rex', 'Rover', 'Henrietta', 'Alan']
  }
});

vm.dogs[2] = 'Bob'
```

There are two ways you can do this instead. You can use `.splice()` to remove the old item and add a new one:

```
vm.dogs.splice(2, 1, 'Bob');
```

Or you can use `Vue.set()` again:

```
Vue.set(vm.dogs, 2, 'Bob');
```

Either way works just as well.

Setting the length of an array

In JavaScript, you can set the length of an array to either pad it to that length with empty items, or to cut off the end of the array (depending on whether the set length is more or less than the old length). You can't do that with an array in the data object, because Vue won't be able to detect any changes to the array.

You can use `splice` instead:

```
vm.dogs.splice(newLength);
```

This works only to shorten the array, not to make it longer.

Two-Way Data Binding

So far you've seen how we can use our data to write to the template and how Vue's reactivity functionality means that when the data is updated, so is the template. That's only one-way data binding, though. If you tried the following, the `inputText` would stay the same, and the text below the input element would stay the same:

```
<div id="app">
  <input type="text" v-bind:value="inputText">
  <p>inputText: {{ inputText }}</p>
</div>
<script>
  new Vue({
    el: '#app',
    data: {
```

```
    inputText: 'initial value'
    }
  });
</script>
```

To get this example to work as expected, you can't use v-bind:value—using v-bind will update the value of the input only when the inputText changes, and not vice versa. Instead, you can use the v-model directive, which works on input elements to bind the value of the input to the corresponding property of the data object so that in addition to the input receiving the initial value of the data, when the input is updated, the data is updated too. Replacing the HTML part of the previous example with the following will now update the inputText: initial value text when you change the value of the input field:

```
<div id="app">
  <input type="text" v-model="inputText">
  <p>inputText: {{ inputText }}</p>
</div>
```

It's important to note that when you use v-model, if you set the value, checked, or selected attributes, they will be ignored. If you want to set the initial value of the input, set it in the data object instead. See the following example:

```
<div id="app">
  <input type="text" v-bind:value="inputText" value="initial value">
  <p>inputText: {{ inputText }}</p>
</div>
<script>
  new Vue({
    el: '#app',
    data: {
      inputText: ''
    }
  });
</script>
```

The inputText will still be bound to the inputText variable, and any text you put in the input box will appear in the paragraph element below it. However, the input will have no initial value, as it was set using the value attribute instead of in the data object, as shown in the first example.

Input elements, multiline text inputs (textareas), select elements, and checkboxes all work basically as expected: the value of the input and the value in the data object are the same (with checkboxes, the value in the data object will be a Boolean value). With radio inputs, it's slightly different, as there is more than one element with the same v-model. The name attribute will be ignored, and the value stored in the data will be equal to the value attribute of the currently selected radio input:

```
<div id="app">
  <label><input type="radio" v-model="value" value="one"> One</label>
```

```
      <label><input type="radio" v-model="value" value="two"> Two</label>
      <label><input type="radio" v-model="value" value="three"> Three</label>

      <p>The value is {{ value }}</p>
    </div>
    <script>
      new Vue({
        el: '#app',
        data: {
          value: 'one'
        }
      });
    </script>
```

When the first checkbox is selected, the value of value is one; when the second is selected, it is two, and so on. Although you can still use the name attribute, Vue will ignore it, and the radio buttons will act normally (with only one being checked at a time) without it.

Setting HTML Dynamically

Sometimes you might want to set the HTML of an element from an expression. Let's say you're calling an API that is returning some HTML which you need to display on the page. In an ideal world, the API would return a JSON object that you could pass to Vue and handle the template yourself, but—it happens. Vue has automatic HTML escaping built in, so if you try to write {{ yourHtml }}, the HTML characters will be escaped—it'll look like <strong>this</strong> in the source—and it will appear as the HTML text sent down from the API on the page. Not ideal!

If you want to take HTML and display it on the page, you can use the v-html directive as follows:

```
    <div v-html="yourHtml"></div>
```

Then, whatever HTML is contained in yourHtml will be written directly to the page without being escaped first.

Be careful with this! By writing HTML to the page from a variable, you are potentially opening yourself up to XSS vulnerabilities.[3] Never put user input in v-html or allow users to modify anything that goes through v-html without carefully validating and escaping what they've written first. You could accidentally allow your users to execute malicious script tags on your site. Use v-html only with data you trust.

---

3 Cross-site scripting (XSS) allows other people to execute abitrary code on your website.

Methods

This section explains how to use methods in Vue to make functions available in your templates in order to perform manipulations on your data.

Functions are pretty neat. They allow us to take a piece of logic and store it in a reusable way so that we can use it multiple times without repeating the code. It's possible to use them in your Vue templates too, as methods. As shown in the following example, storing a function as a property of the methods object makes it available in your templates:

```
<div id="app">
  <p>Current status: {{ statusFromId(status) }}</p>
</div>
<script>
  new Vue({
    el: '#app',
    data: {
      status: 2
    },
    methods: {
      statusFromId(id) {
        const status = ({
          0: 'Asleep',
          1: 'Eating',
          2: 'Learning Vue'
        })[id];

        return status || 'Unknown status: ' + id;
      }
    }
  });
</script>
```

This turns a number representing the status—possibly supplied in another step by an API—into a human-readable string indicating the actual status. You can add methods by specifying them as properties of the methods object.

In addition to being able to use methods in interpolations, you can use them in bound attributes—and really, anywhere that you can use JavaScript expressions. Here's a short example:

```
<div id="app">
  <ul>
    <li v-for="number in filterPositive(numbers)">{{ number }}</li>
  </ul>
</div>
<script>
  new Vue({
    el: '#app',
    data: {
```

```
      numbers: [-5, 0, 2, -1, 1, 0.5]
    },
    methods: {
      filterPositive(numbers) {
        return numbers.filter((number) => number >= 0);
      }
    }
  });
</script>
```

The method takes an array and returns a new array with all the negative numbers removed, so in this example, we get a list of positive numbers output to the page.

We looked at reactivity previously, and you'll be glad to know that it applies here too. If numbers is changed—for example, if a number is added or removed—the method will be called again with the new numbers, and the information outputted to the page will be updated.

this

In a method, this refers to the component that the method is attached to. You can access properties on the data object and other methods by using this:

```
<div id="app">
  <p>The sum of the positive numbers is {{ getPositiveNumbersSum() }}</p>
</div>
<script>
  new Vue({
    el: '#app',
    data: {
      numbers: [-5, 0, 2, -1, 1, 0.5]
    },
    methods: {
      getPositiveNumbers() {
        // Note that we're now using this.numbers
        // to refer directly to the data object.
        return this.numbers.filter((number) => number >= 0);
      },
      getPositiveNumbersSum() {
        return this.getPositiveNumbers().reduce((sum, val) => sum + val);
      }
    }
  });
</script>
```

Here, this.numbers in getPositiveNumbers refers to the numbers array in the data object that we were previously passing in as an argument; this.getPositiveNum bers() refers to the other method with that name.

You'll see in future sections that you can access other things by using this too.

Computed Properties

Computed properties sit halfway between properties of the data object and methods: you can access them as if they were properties of the data object, but they are specified as functions.

Check out the following example, which takes the data stored as numbers, adds them all together, and outputs the total to the page:

```
<div id="app">
  <p>Sum of numbers: {{ numberTotal }}</p>
</div>
<script>
  new Vue({
    el: '#app',
    data: {
      numbers: [5, 8, 3]
    },
    computed: {
      numberTotal() {
        return numbers.reduce((sum, val) => sum + val);
      }
    }
  });
</script>
```

Although we could write the entire statement to calculate the total in the template, it's much more convenient and readable to have it defined elsewhere. We can also access it in methods, other computed properties, and anywhere else in the component by using this. As with methods, when numbers changes, numberTotal changes too, and the change is reflected in the template.

But what's the difference between using computed properties and methods, aside from the obvious syntax difference? Well, there are a couple.

The first is that computed properties are cached: if you call a method multiple times in a template, the code inside the method will be run every single time the method is called, whereas if a computed property is called multiple times, the code inside will be run only once, and every time after that, the cached value will be used. The code will be run again only when a dependency of the method changes: for example, in the previous code sample, if we push a new item to basketItems, the code inside basket Total is run again to get the new value. This is good if you're doing something potentially resource intensive, as it ensures that the code will not be run more than necessary.

You can see this behavior by adding a console.log() statement to a computed property that is repeatedly called. You can observe that the console.log() statement, and thus the entire computed property, is evaluated only when the value changes:

```
<script>
  new Vue({
    el: '#app',
    data: () => ({
      value: 10,
    }),
    computed: {
      doubleValue() {
        console.log('doubleValue computed property changed');

        return this.value * 2;
      }
    }
  });
</script>
```

The string will be logged to the console only once when the app is initialized and once every time `value` changes.

The other difference between computed properties and methods is that in addition to being able to get values of computed properties, as shown in the previous example, it's possible to set values on computed properties and do something with the set value. You can do that by changing the computed property from a function to an object with `get` and `set` properties. For example, let's say we want to add the ability to add new items to the `numbers` array by adding or subtracting them from `numberTotal`. We can do that by adding a setter that will compare the new value to the old value, and then append the difference to the `numbers` array:

```
<div id="app">
  <p>Sum of numbers: {{ numberTotal }}</p>
</div>
<script>
  new Vue({
    el: '#app',
    data: {
      numbers: [5, 8, 3]
    },
    computed: {
      numberTotal: {
        get() {
          return numbers.reduce((sum, val) => sum + val);
        },
        set(newValue) {
          const oldValue = this.numberTotal;
          const difference = newValue - oldValue;
          this.numbers.push(difference).
        }
      }
    }
  });
</script>
```

Now, calling `this.numberTotal += 5` somewhere else in the component will cause the number 5 to be added to the end of the `numbers` array—neat!

The Data Object, Methods, or Computed Properties?

You've met the data object, where you can store data such as strings, arrays, and objects in an object; you've met methods, where you can store functions and call them from your templates; and you've met computed properties, where you can store functions and call them as if they were properties in the data object. But which should you use, and when?

Each has its uses and is best used in combination with one another, but some of them are better for certain tasks than others. For example, if you're accepting an argument, you definitely want to use a method, not data or a computed property: neither of them can accept arguments.

The data object is best for pure data: you want to put data somewhere to use in your template or in a method or computed property, and you want to leave it there. You might update it later.

Methods are best when you want to add functions to your templates: you pass them data, and they do something with that data and possibly return different data.

Computed properties are best for performing more-complicated expressions that you wouldn't want to be using in your template because they're too long or you'd have to repeat yourself too often. They usually work with other computed properties or your data. They're basically like an extended, more powerful version of the data object.

You can compare the different ways of working with data—the data object, methods, and computed properties—in Table 1-1.

Table 1-1. The data object versus methods versus computed properties

	Readable?	Writable?	Accepts arguments?	Computed?	Cached?
The data object	Yes	Yes	No	No	N/A, as it's not computed
Methods	Yes	No	Yes	Yes	No
Computed properties	Yes	Yes	No	Yes	Yes

This may look daunting, but it's something that's easy to get a hang of through use!

Watchers

Watchers allow us to watch a property of the data object or a computed property for changes.

If you're coming to Vue from another framework, you may have been wondering how to watch something for changes and waiting for this feature. Be careful, though! In Vue, there's usually a better way to do something than to use a watcher—usually, using a computed property. For example, instead of setting data and then watching it for changes, using a computed property with a setter is a much better way to do it.

Watchers are easy to use: just specify the name of the property to watch. For example, to watch this.count for changes:

```
<script>
  new Vue({
    el: '#app',
    data: {
      count: 0
    },
    watchers: {
      count() {
        // this.count has been changed!
      }
    }
  });
</script>
```

Although most simple examples don't require watchers, they are good for performing asynchronous operations. For example, let's say we have an input that a user can type in, but we want to display on the page what was in the input five seconds ago. To do that, you can use v-model to sync the value of the input to your data object, and then watch that value for changes and in the watcher write the value to another property of the data object after a delay:

```
<div id="app">
  <input type="text" v-model="inputValue">

  <p>Five seconds ago, the input said "{{ oldInputValue }}".</p>
</div>
<script>
  new Vue({
    el: '#app',
    data: {
      inputValue: '',
      oldInputValue: ''
    },
    watch: {
      inputValue() {
        const newValue = this.inputValue;
```

```
        setTimeout(() => {
          this.oldInputValue = newValue;
        }, 5000);
      }
    }
  });
</script>
```

Note that in this example, we're writing this.inputValue to a variable local to that function: this is because otherwise, when the function given to setTimeout is called, this.inputValue will have updated to the latest value!

Watching Properties of Objects in the Data Object

Sometimes you might have a whole object stored in your data object. To watch a property of that object for changes, you can specify the watcher name with dots in it, as if you were reading the object:

```
new Vue({
  data: {
    formData: {
      username: ''
    }
  },
  watch: {
    'formData.username'() {
      // this.formData.username has changed
    }
  }
});
```

Getting the Old Value

Watchers are passed two arguments when their watched property is changed: the new value of the watched property, and the old value. This can be useful for seeing what has changed:

```
watch: {
  inputValue(val, oldVal) {
    console.log(val, oldVal);
  }
}
```

val equals (in this case) this.inputValue. I usually find myself using the latter instead.

Deep Watching

When watching an object, you might want to watch the entire object for changes, not just the property. By default, the watcher won't fire if you're watching formData and you modify formData.username; it will fire only if you replace the entire formData property.

Watching the entire object is known as a *deep watch*, and we can tell Vue to do this by setting the deep option to true:

```
watch: {
  formData: {
    handler() {
      console.log(val, oldVal);
    },
    deep: true
  }
}
```

Filters

Filters, also often seen in other templating languages, are a convenient way of manipulating data in your templates. I find them great for making simple display changes to strings and numbers: for example, changing a string to the correct case or displaying a number in a human-readable format.

Take the following code sample:

```
<div id="app">
  <p>Product one cost: ${{ (productOneCost / 100).toFixed(2) }}</p>
  <p>Product two cost: ${{ (productTwoCost / 100).toFixed(2) }}</p>
  <p>Product three cost: ${{ (productThreeCost / 100).toFixed(2) }}</p>
</div>
<script>
  new Vue({
    el: '#app',
    data: {
      productOneCost: 998,
      productTwoCost: 2399,
      productThreeCost: 5300
    }
  });
</script>
```

It works, but there's a lot of duplication. For every item, we're doing the math to convert it from cents to dollars, displaying it to two decimal places, and adding the dollar sign. Although we can definitely split that logic into a method, this time we'll split that logic into a filter, as it's more readable and can be added globally:

```
<div id="app">
  <p>Product one cost: {{ productOneCost | formatCost }}</p>
  <p>Product two cost: {{ productTwoCost | formatCost }}</p>
  <p>Product three cost: {{ productThreeCost | formatCost }}</p>
</div>
<script>
  new Vue({
    el: '#app',
    data: {
      productOneCost: 998,
      productTwoCost: 2399,
      productThreeCost: 5300
    },
    filters: {
      formatCost(value) {
        return '$' + (value / 100).toFixed(2);
      }
    }
  });
</script>
```

That's a lot better—much less duplication, much easier to read, and much more maintainable. Now if we decide we want to add logic to it—say, we want to add currency conversion functionality—we have to do it only once instead of changing the code every place it is used.

You can use multiple filters in the same expression by chaining them together. For example, if we have a round filter that rounds a number to the nearest integer, you could use both filters together by writing {{ productOneCost | round | format Cost }}. The round filter would be called first, and then the value returned by that filter would be passed to the formatCost filter and output to the page.

Filters can also take arguments. In the following example, the given string would be passed into the filter function as the second argument:

```
<div id="app">
  <p>Product one cost: {{ productOneCost | formatCost('$') }}</p>
</div>
<script>
  new Vue({
    el: '#app',
    data: {
      productOneCost: 998,
    },
    filters: {
      formatCost(value, symbol) {
        return symbol + (value / 100).toFixed(2);
      }
    }
  });
</script>
```

In addition to working with interpolation, you can use filters with `v-bind` when binding values to arguments:

```
<div id="app">
  <input type="text" v-bind:value="productCost | formatCost('$')">
</div>
```

You can also use `Vue.filter()` to register filters instead of on a per-component basis:

```
Vue.filter('formatCost', function (value, symbol) {
  return symbol + (val / 100).toFixed(2);
});
```

This is good for registering filters that you're going to use all over your app. I generally stick all of my filters in a separate file called *filters.js*.

Using filters carries two small caveats. The first is that filters are the only place where you can't use this to refer to methods and data on the components. This is intentional: it's because filters are supposed to be pure functions, meaning that the function takes input and returns the same output every time without referring to any external data. If you want to access other data in a filter, pass it in as an argument.

The other caveat is that you can use filters only in interpolations and `v-bind` directives. In Vue 1, it was possible to use them anywhere you could use expressions; for example, in `v-for` directives:

```
<li v-for="item in items | filterItems">{{ item }}</li>
```

This is no longer the case in Vue 2, and you'll have to use a method or computed property in the preceding case.

Accessing Elements Directly Using ref

Sometimes you might find yourself needing to access an element directly in the DOM; maybe you're using a third-party library that isn't written to work with Vue, or maybe you want to do something that Vue can't quite handle itself. You can use `ref` to access the element directly without having to use `querySelector` or one of the other native ways to select an element from the DOM.

To access an element using a ref, set the `ref` attribute of the element to a string that you can access the element using:

```
<canvas ref="myCanvas"></canvas>
```

Then in your JavaScript, the element will be stored on the `this.$refs` object as whatever you set the `ref` attribute to. In this case, you can access it by using `this.$refs.myCanvas`.

Using `ref` is especially useful in components. It's possible that the same code could appear multiple times in the same page, meaning that you can't add a unique class and use `querySelector` at all. `this.$refs` contains only the refs for the current component, meaning that if you call `this.$refs.blablabla` in a component, it will always refer to the element in that component, not anywhere else in the document.

Inputs and Events

Until this point, pretty much everything you've seen has been about displaying data—we haven't made anything that interactive yet. Now, I'll introduce you to event binding in Vue.

To bind an event listener to an element, you can use the `v-on` directive. It takes the name of the event as the argument, and the event listener as the passed value. For example, to increase the value of `counter` by one when a button is clicked, you can write the following:

```
<button v-on:click="counter++">Click to increase counter</button>
<p>You've clicked the button {{ counter }}</p> times.
```

You can also provide the name of a method that will be called when the button is clicked:

```
<div id="app">
  <button v-on:click="increase">Click to increase counter</button>
  <p>You've clicked the button {{ counter }}</p> times.
</div>

<script>
  new Vue({
    el: '#app',
    data: {
      counter: 0
    },
    methods: {
      increase(e) {
        this.counter++;
      }
    }
  });
</script>
```

That works the same as the previous example.

One significant difference between using a method and putting the code inline is that if you use a method, the event object is passed in as the first argument. This event object is the native DOM event that you would get if you had added the event listener by using JavaScript's built-in `.addEventListener()` method and can be useful, for getting the `keyCode` of a keyboard event, for example.

You can access the event when writing code inline, too, as the $event variable. This can be useful when you're adding the same event listener to multiple elements and want to know which one it was triggered from.

The v-on Shortcut

Similarly to the v-bind directive, v-on also has a shorter way of writing it. Instead of writing v-on:click, you can write just @click.

This is the same as the previous example:

```
<button @click="increase">Click to increase counter</button>
```

I nearly always use the short version instead of writing v-on.

Event Modifiers

You can also do a load of things to modify the event handler or the event itself.

To prevent the default action of the event from happening—for example, to stop a page navigation from happening when a link is clicked—you can use the .prevent modifier:

```
<a @click.prevent="handleClick">...</a>
```

To stop the event from propagating so that the event isn't triggered on the parent elements, you can use the .stop modifier:

```
<button @click.stop="handleClick">...</button>
```

To have the event listener be triggered only the first time the event is fired, you can use the .once modifier:

```
<button @click.once="handleFirstClick">...</button>
```

To use capture mode, meaning that the event will be triggered on this element before it is dispatched on the elements below it in the tree (versus bubble mode, in which it's fired on the element first and then bubbles up the DOM), you can use the .capture modifier:

```
<div @click.capture="handleCapturedClick">...</div>
```

To trigger the handler when the event was triggered on the element itself, not a child element (basically, when event.target is the element the handler is being added to) you can use the .self modifier:

```
<div @click.self="handleSelfClick">...</div>
```

You can also specify just the event and modifier without giving it a value, and you can chain modifiers together. For example, the following will stop a click event from propagating any further down the tree—but only the first time:

```
<div @click.stop.capture.once></div>
```

In addition to those event modifiers, there are also key modifiers. These are used on keyboard events so that you can fire the event only when a certain key is pressed. Consider the following:

```
<div id="app">
  <form @keyup="handleKeyup">...</form>
</div>

<script>
  new Vue({
    el: '#app',
    methods: {
      handleKeyup(e) {
        if (e.keyCode === 27) {
          // do something
        }
      }
    }
  });
</script>
```

The code inside the if statement will run only when the key with keyCode 27—the Escape key—is pressed. However, Vue has a way to do this built in as a modifier. You can specify the key code as the modifier, like so:

```
<form @keyup.27="handleEscape">...</form>
```

Now, handleEscape will be be triggered only when the Escape key is pressed. Aliases are also available for the most used keys: .enter, .tab, .delete, .esc, .space, .up, .down, .left, and .right. Instead of writing @keyup.27 and having to remember which key 27 is, you can just write @keyup.esc.

As of Vue 2.5.0, you can use any key name from the key property of the event. For example, when you press the left Shift key, e.key equals ShiftLeft. To listen for when the Shift key is released, you can use the following:

```
<form @keyup.shift-left="handleShiftLeft">...</form>
```

Similar to the key modifiers, three mouse button modifiers can be added to mouse events: .left, .middle, and .right.

Some modifiers exist for modifier keys such as Ctrl and Shift: .ctrl, .alt, .shift, and .meta. The first three modifiers are fairly self-explanatory, but .meta is less clear: on Windows, it's the Windows key, and on macOS, it is the Command key.

Finally, an .exact operator will trigger the event handler only if the specified keys and no other keys are pressed. For example:

```
<input @keydown.enter.exact="handleEnter">
```

That will fire when Enter is pressed, but not when any other keys—for example, Command-Enter or Ctrl-Enter—are pressed.

Life-Cycle Hooks

You've seen a couple of times now that if you specify a function as the created property on a component or your Vue instance, it is called when the component is, well, created. This is an example of what's known as a *life-cycle hook*, a series of functions that are called at various points throughout the life cycle of a component—all the way from when it created and added the DOM, to when it is destroyed.

Vue has eight life-cycle hooks, but they're pretty easy to remember because four of them are just *before* hooks that are fired before the other ones.

Here's the basic life cycle of an object: first, the Vue instance is initiated when new Vue() is called. The first hook, beforeCreate, is called, and reactivity is initiated. Then the created hook is called—you can see how this works with the hook names. The "before" hook is called before the thing that triggers the hook happens, and then the actual hook is called afterward. Next, the template is compiled—either from the template or render options, or from the outerHTML of the element that Vue was initialized to. The DOM element is now ready to be created, so the beforeMount hook is fired, the element is created, and then the mounted hook is fired.

One thing to be careful of is that as of Vue 2.0, the mounted hook doesn't guarantee that the element has been added to the DOM. To make sure that it has been added, you can call Vue.nextTick() (also available as this.$nextTick()) with a callback method containing the code you want to run after the element is definitely added to the DOM. For example:

```
<div id="app">
  <p>Hello world</p>
</div>

<script>
  new Vue({
    el: '#app',
    mounted() {
      // Element might not have been added to the DOM yet

      this.$nextTick(() => {
        // Element has definitely been added to the DOM now
      });
    }
  });
</script>
```

Four hooks have been fired so far, as the instance is initialized and then added to the DOM, and our users can now see our component. Maybe our data updates, though, so the DOM is updated to reflect that change. Before the change is made, another hook is fired, `beforeUpdate`, and afterward, the `updated` hook is fired. This hook can be fired multiple times as multiple changes to the DOM are made.

Finally, we've witnessed the creation and life of our component, but it's time for it to go. Before it is removed from the DOM, the `beforeDestroy` hook is fired, and after it has been removed, the `destroyed` hook is fired.

Those are all the hooks that are fired throughout the life cycle of a Vue instance. Here they are again, but this time from the point of view of the hooks, not the instance:

- `beforeCreate` is fired before the instance is initialized.
- `created` is fired after the instance has been initialized but before it is added to the DOM.
- `beforeMount` is fired after the element is ready to be added to the DOM but before it has been.
- `mounted` is fired after the element has been created (but not necessarily added to the DOM: use `nextTick` for that).
- `beforeUpdate` is fired when there are changes to be made to the DOM output.
- `updated` is fired after changes have been written to the DOM.
- `beforeDestroy` is fired when the component is about to be destroyed and removed from the DOM.
- `destroyed` is fired after the component has been destroyed.

While there do seem to be a lot of hooks, you have to remember only four (`created`, `mounted`, `updated`, and `destroyed`), and you can work out the other four from there.

Custom Directives

In addition to the built-in directives such as `v-if`, `v-model`, and `v-html`, it's possible to create your own custom directives. Directives are great for times when you want to do something directly with the DOM—if you find that you're not accessing the DOM, you'd probably be better off with a component instead.

As a simple example, let's build a `v-blink` directive, which simulates the behavior of the `<blink>` tag. We'll be able to use it like this:

```
<p v-blink>This content will blink</p>
```

Adding a directive is similar to adding a filter: you can pass it in the `directives` property of your Vue instance or component, or else you can register it globally using `Vue.directive()`. You pass the name of the directive, plus an object containing hook functions that are run at various points through the life of the element the directive has been added to.

The five hook functions are bind, inserted, update, componentUpdated, and unbind. I'll explain them all in moment, but for now we're just going to use the bind hook, which is called when the directive is bound to the element. In the hook, we'll toggle the visibility of the element once a second:

```
Vue.directive('blink', {
  bind(el) {
    let isVisible = true;
    setInterval(() => {
      isVisible = !isVisible;
      el.style.visibility = isVisible ? 'visible' : 'hidden';
    }, 1000);
  }
});
```

Now, any element the directive is applied to will blink once a second—just what we wanted.

Directives have multiple hook functions, just as the Vue instance and components have life-cycle hooks. They're named differently and don't do exactly the same thing as the life-cycle hooks, so let's go through what they do now:

- The bind hook is called when the directive is bound to the element.
- The inserted hook is called when the bound element has been inserted into its parent node—but just as with mounted, this doesn't guarantee that the element has been added to the document yet. Use this.$nextTick for that.
- The update hook is called when the parent of the component the directive is bound to is updated, but possibly before the component's children have updated.
- The componentUpdated hook is similar to the update hook, but is called after the component's children have updated too.
- The unbind hook is used for teardown, and is called when the directive is unbound from the element.

You don't have to call all the hooks every time. In fact, they're all optional, so you don't have to call any of them.

I find myself most commonly using the bind and update hooks. Conveniently, if you want to use just those two hooks, there's a shorthand way of doing it—you can omit the object and specify a function that will be used as both hooks, as the argument:

```
Vue.directive('my-directive', (el) => {
  // This code will run both on "bind" and "update"
});
```

Hook Arguments

You've seen before that directives accept arguments (v-bind:class), modifiers (v-on.once), and values (v-if="expression"). It's possible to access all of these by using the second argument passed to the hook function, binding.

If using v-my-directive:example.one.two="someExpression" to call our directive, the binding object will contain the following properties:

- The name property is the name of the directive without the v-. In this case, it's my-directive.

- The value property is the value passed to the directive. In this case, it would be whatever someExpression evaluates to. For example, if the data object were equal to { someExpression: *hello world* }, value would equal hello world.

- The oldValue property is the previous value passed to the directive. It's available only in update and componentUpdated. With our example, if we had a different value for someExpression, the update hook would be called with the new value as value and the old value as oldValue.

- The expression property is the value of the attribute as a string before evaluation. In this case, it would literally be someExpression.

- The arg property is the argument passed to the directive; in this case, example.

- The modifiers property is an object containing any modifiers passed to the directive. In this case, it will equal { one: true, two: true }.

To demonstrate how to use an argument, let's modify our hook directive to take an argument indicating how quickly the element should blink:

```
Vue.directive('blink', {
  bind(el, binding) {
    let isVisible = true;
    setInterval(() => {
      isVisible = !isVisible;
      el.style.visibility = isVisible ? 'visible' : 'hidden';
    }, binding.value || 1000);
  }
});
```

I've added the binding argument, and changed the timing on the setInterval to binding.value || 1000 instead of just 1000. This example is lacking any logic to update the component if the argument changes, though. In order to do that, we'd need to store the ID returned by setInterval on a data attribute on the object and cancel the old interval before creating a new one in the update hook.

Transitions and Animations

Vue contains a plethora of functionality that you can use to power animations and transitions in your Vue apps—from helping you with CSS transitions and JavaScript animations when elements enter or leave the page or are modified, to transitioning between components and even animating the data itself. There's far too much to cover in a general book on Vue, so I'll focus on the stuff I've found myself using most frequently, and you can check out the Vue documentation on transitions (with some really cool demos!) yourself later.

To start, let's look at the `<transition>` component and how to use it with CSS transitions to animate elements in and out of our document.

CSS Transitions

CSS transitions are good for simple animations, in which you're just transitioning one or more CSS properties from one value to another. For example, you can transition `color` from `blue` to `red`, or `opacity` from `1` to `0`. Vue provides a `<transition>` component that adds classes to a contained element with a `v-if` directive, which you can use to apply CSS transitions when an element is added or removed.

Throughout this section, we'll be referring to the following template, which has a button, and an element that toggles visibility when the button is pressed:

```
<div id="app">
  <button @click="divVisible = !divVisible">Toggle visibility</button>

  <div v-if="divVisible">This content is sometimes hidden</div>
</div>
<script>
  new Vue({
    el: '#app',
    data: {
      divVisible: true
    }
  });
</script>
```

Currently if you click the button, the content in the `div` element will be immediately hidden and shown again, with no transition.

Let's say we want to add a simple transition to it: we want it to fade in and out when the visibility is toggled. To do that, we can wrap the `div` in a transition component, like so:

```
<transition name="fade">
  <div v-if="divVisible">This content is sometimes hidden</div>
</transition>
```

That by itself won't do anything (it will behave exactly the way it did before we added the `<transition>` element), but if we add the following CSS, we'll get our fade transition:

```css
.fade-enter-active, .fade-leave-active {
  transition: opacity .5s;
}
.fade-enter, .fade-leave-to {
  opacity: 0;
}
```

Now, when you click the button to toggle visibility, the element fades in and out of the page instead of being added or removed instantly as it was before.

The way that this works is that Vue takes the name of the transition and uses it to add classes to the contained element at various points through the transition. Two types of transition, enter and leave, are applied when the element is added and removed from the document, respectively. The classes are as follows:

{name}-enter

This class is applied to the element as it is added to the DOM, and immediately removed after one frame. Use it to set CSS properties that you want to be removed as the element transitions in.

{name}-enter-active

This class is applied to the element for the entirety of the animation. It's added at the same time the -enter class is added, and removed after the animation has completed. This class is good for setting the CSS transition property, containing the length of the transition, the properties to transition, and the easings to use.

{name}-enter-to

This class is added to the element at the same time as the -enter class is removed. It's good for setting CSS properties that are added as the element transitions in, but I generally find it's better to transition the inverse of the property on the -enter class instead.

{name}-leave

This class is the equivalent of the -enter class for the leave transitions. It's added when the leave transition is triggered and then removed after one frame. Much like the -enter-to class, this class isn't that useful; it's better to animate the inverse by using -leave-to instead.

{name}-leave-active

This class is the equivalent of -enter-active, but for the leave transitions. It's applied for the entire duration of the exit transition.

`{name}-leave-to`
> This class is once again the equivalent of `-enter-to`, but for the leave transitions. It's applied one frame after the transition starts (when `-leave` is removed) and remains until the end of the transition.

In practice, I find myself using these four classes the most:

`{name}-enter`
> This class sets CSS properties to transition during the enter transition.

`{name}-enter-active`
> This class sets the `transition` CSS property for the enter transition.

`{name}-leave-active`
> This class sets the `transition` CSS property for the leave transition.

`{name}-leave-to`
> This class sets CSS properties to transition during the leave transition.

So the way the previous code example works is that both the enter and leave transitions are `.5s` long, and `opacity` is transitioned (with the default easing), and both on enter and leave we are transitioning to and from `opacity: 0`. We're fading the element in when it enters the document, and fading it out when it leaves again.

JavaScript Animations

In addition to CSS animations, the `<transition>` component provides hooks that you can use to power JavaScript animations. Using these hooks, you can write animations by using either your own code or a library such as GreenSock or Velocity.

The hooks are similar to their counterparts for CSS transitions:

`before-enter`
> This hook is fired before the enter animation starts and is good for setting initial values.

`enter`
> This hook is fired when the enter animation starts and is where you can run the animation from. You can use a done callback to indicate when the animation has finished.

`afterEnter`
> This hook is fired when the enter animation has ended.

`enterCancelled`
> This hook is fired when the enter animation is cancelled.

`beforeLeave`

This hook is the leave equivalent of `before-enter`, and is fired before the leave animation starts.

`leave`

This hook is the leave equivalent of `enter` and is where you can run the animation from.

`afterLeave`

This hook is fired when the leave animation has ended.

`leaveCancelled`

This hook is fired when the leave animation is cancelled.

These hooks are triggered on the `<transition>` element as events, like so:

```
<transition
  v-on:before-enter="handleBeforeEnter"
  v-on:enter="handleEnter"
  v-on:leave="handleLeave>
  <div v-if="divVisible">...</div>
</transition>
```

With those event handlers added, we can add the same effect as in the CSS transition example, but using GreenSock instead, like this:

```
new Vue({
  el: '#app',
  data: {
    divVisible: false
  },
  methods: {
    handleBeforeEnter(el) {
      el.style.opacity = 0;
    },
    handleEnter(el, done) {
      TweenLite.to(el, 0.6, { opacity: 1, onComplete: done });
    },
    handleLeave(el, done) {
      TweenLite.to(el, 0.6, { opacity: 0, onComplete: done });
    }
  }
});
```

Using JavaScript animations, we can create much more complicated animations than we can with CSS transitions, including multiple steps, or a different transition every time. CSS transitions are generally more performant, though, so stick with them unless you need functionality you can't get with just CSS transitions.

Now that we've explored some of the basic things that you can do with Vue, let's look at how you can structure your code by using components.

Summary

In this chapter we looked at some of the basics of using Vue:

- We looked at some of the reasons to use Vue.
- We looked at how you can install and set up Vue using either a CDN or webpack.
- We looked at the syntax of Vue: how you can use templates, the data object and directives to display your data on the page.
- We looked at the difference between the v-if and v-show directives.
- We looked at how you can use the v-for directive to loop in templates.
- We looked at how you can use v-bind to bind a property of the data object to an HTML attribute.
- We looked at how Vue automatically updates the value displayed on the page when the data updates: this is called reactivity.
- We looked at two-way data binding: using v-model to both display data in an input and update the data object when the value of the input is changed.
- We looked at how you can use v-html to set the inner HTML of an element from the data object.
- We looked at how you can use methods to make functions available to your templates and throughout your Vue instance. We also looked at what this means inside a method.
- We looked at how you can use computed properties to create values that you can access as if they are properties of the data object, but that are computed at runtime and specified as functions.
- We looked at how you can use watchers to watch properties of the data object or computed properties and do something when they change—but it's generally a good idea to avoid watchers and use computed properties instead.
- We looked at filters, a convinient way of manipulating data in your templates— useful for formatting data, for example.
- We looked at how you can access elements directly using ref, which is useful if you're using a third-party library that doesn't work great with Vue, or if you want to do something that Vue itself can't handle.
- We looked at event binding using v-on, or the short syntax using @ followed by the event name.
- We looked at the life-cycle of a Vue instance and how you can use hooks to execute code on them.
- We looked at how you can create your own custom directives.

- We looked at how Vue provides functionality to work with CSS transitions and JavaScript animations.

CHAPTER 2

Components in Vue.js

You've seen me mention components a couple of times now, but what is a component? A *component* is a self-contained piece of code that represents a part of the page. Components have their own data, their own JavaScript, and often their own styling. They can contain other components, and they can communicate with each other. A component could be something as small as a button or an icon, or it could be something bigger, such as a form you reuse a lot throughout your site or an entire page.

The main advantage of separating your code into components is that the code responsible for each bit of the page is close to the rest of the code for that component. No more having to search for a selector in a ton of JavaScript files to see what is adding that event listener; the JavaScript is right there next to the HTML! Because components are self-contained, you also can make sure that none of the code inside a component will affect any other components or have any side effects.

Component Basics

Let's dive right in and demonstrate a simple component:

```
const CustomButton = {
  template: '<button>Custom button</button>'
};
```

That's it. You can then pass this component into your app by using the components objects:

```
<div id="app">
  <custom-button></custom-button>
</div>
<script>
  const CustomButton = {
    template: '<button>Custom button</button>'
```

```
    };

    new Vue({
      el: '#app',
      components: {
        CustomButton
      }
    });
  </script>
```

This outputs the custom button to the page.

You can also register components globally using the Vue.component() method, as follows:

```
Vue.component('custom-button', {
  template: '<button>Custom button</button>'
});
```

You can then use the component the same way it was used in the previous example in the template, but you don't need to specify it in the components object anymore; it's available everywhere.

Data, Methods, and Computed Properties

Each component can have its own data, methods, computed properties, and everything you've seen previously—just like the Vue instance itself. The object to define a component is similar to the object we used to define the Vue instance, and you can use it the same in a lot of ways. For example, let's define and globally register a component with some data and a computed property:

```
Vue.component('positive-numbers', {
  template: '<p>{{ positiveNumbers.length }} positive numbers</p>',
  data() {
    return {
      numbers: [-5, 0, 2, -1, 1, 0.5]
    };
  },
  computed: {
    positiveNumbers() {
      return this.numbers.filter((number) => number >= 0);
    }
  }
});
```

We can then use it as <positive-numbers></positive-numbers> anywhere in our Vue templates.

You might have noticed one subtle difference between a component and the Vue instance: whereas the data property on your Vue instance is an object, the data property on components is a function. This is because you can use a component multiple times on the same page, and you probably don't want them sharing a data object—imagine if you clicked a button, and the button on the other side of the page responded as well! For this reason, the data property should be a function that Vue will call when the component is initialized in order to generate the data object. If you forget to make the data property a function on a component, Vue will throw a warning.

Passing in Data

Components are useful, but they really show their power when you start passing data into them. You can pass data into a component by using *props*. Take the following example:

```
<div id="app">
  <color-preview color="red"></color-preview>
  <color-preview color="blue"></color-preview>
</div>
<script>
  Vue.component('color-preview', {
    template: '<div class="color-preview" :style="style"></div>',
    props: ['color'],
    computed: {
      style() {
        return { backgroundColor: this.color };
      }
    }
  });

  new Vue({
    el: '#app'
  });
</script>
```

The props are passed into the components as attributes on the HTML (color="red", for example); then in the component, the *props* property indicates the names of the props that can be passed into the component—in this case, just a color. Then in the component we can access the value of the prop by using this.color.

The HTML output for the preceding code is as follows:

```
<div id="app">
  <div class="color-preview" style="background-color: red"></div>
  <div class="color-preview" style="background-color: blue"></div>
</div>
```

Prop Validation

Instead of passing in a simple array containing the names of the props your component can receive, it's also possible to pass an object containing information about the props, such as their types, whether they're required, default values, and custom validator functions for more advanced validation.

To specify the type of a prop, pass it a native constructor such as `Number`, `String`, or `Object`, or a custom constructor function that will be checked with `instanceof`. For example:

```
Vue.component('price-display', {
  props: {
    price: Number,
    unit: String
  }
});
```

If price is anything other than a number, or unit is anything other than a string, Vue will throw a warning.

If a prop can be one of multiple types, you can pass in all the valid types in an array, such as `price: [Number, String, Price]` (where `Price` is a custom constructor function).

You can also specify whether a prop is required, or give it a default value if one isn't specified. To do that, specify an object instead of a constructor as before, and pass in the type as the `type` property of that object:

```
Vue.component('price-display', {
  props: {
    price: {
      type: Number,
      required: true
    },
    unit: {
      type: String,
      default: '$'
    }
  }
});
```

In that example, `price` is a required prop, and a warning will be thrown if it isn't specified. `unit` isn't required, but has a default value of $, so if you don't pass in any value, `this.unit` will equal $ inside the component.

Finally, you can pass in a validator function that will be passed the value of the prop and should return `true` if the prop is valid, or `false` if it is not. For example, the following example validates whether the number is above zero so that you can't accidentally give things negative prices:

```
price: {
  type: Number,
  required: true,
  validator(value) {
```

```
      return value >= 0;
    }
  }
```

Casing of Props

Vue handles the casing of props in a nice way: you probably want to use kebab case (my-prop="") only in your HTML, but you probably don't want to refer to your props as this[my-prop] in your JavaScript. Camel case (this.myProp) is much nicer to type and read.

Luckily, Vue handles this for you. Props specified as kebab case in your HTML are automatically converted to camel case in your component:

```
<div id="app">
  <price-display percentage-discount="20%"></price-display>
</div>
<script>
  Vue.component('price-display', {
    props: {
      percentageDiscount: Number
    }
  });

  new Vue({
    el: '#app'
  });
</script>
```

That works as expected without having to do any work ourselves.

Reactivity

You've seen that when the value of the data object, method, or computed property changes, the template is updated too, and this also works for props. v-bind can be used when setting the prop on the parent to bind it to a value, and then whenever that value changes, anywhere it is used in the component is also updated.

For a simple example of this, let's make a component that displays a number given to it as a prop:

```
Vue.component('display-number', {
  template: '<p>The number is {{ number }}</p>',
  props: {
    number: {
      type: Number,
      required: true
    }
  }
});
```

Then let's display this on the page with a value that increases by one every second:

```
<div id="app">
  <display-number v-bind:number="number"></display-number>
</div>
<script>
  new Vue({
    el: '#app',
    data: {
      number: 0
    },
    created() {
      setInterval(() => {
        this.number++;
      }, 1000);
    }
  });
</script>
```

The number passed to the display-number component is increasing by one every second (remember, the created function runs when the instance is created), and so the prop is changing once a second. Vue is clever enough to know this, and so it updates the page.

Using v-bind is required when passing in anything other than strings. The following will throw a warning:

```
<display-number number="10"></display-number>
```

This is because the value is being passed in as a string, not a number. To pass the number in, add v-bind to evaluate it as an expression before it is passed in:

```
<display-number v-bind:number="10"></display-number>
```

Data Flow and the .sync Modifier

Data is passed to a child from a parent via a prop, and when that data is updated in the parent, the prop passed to the child is updated. However, you cannot modify the prop from the child component. This is known as a *one-way-down binding*, and prevents components from perhaps unintentionally mutating a parent's state.

However, two-way data binding can be useful in some cases. If you want to use two-way data binding, you can use a modifier to achieve it: the .sync modifier. It's just syntactical sugar. Take the following code:

```
<count-from-number
  :number.sync="numberToDisplay"
/>
```

This code is the equivalent of the following:

```
<count-from-number
  :number="numberToDisplay"
  @update:number="val => numberToDisplay = val"
  />
```

So, in order to change the value in the parent component, you need to emit the update:number event, where the argument—in this case, number—is the name of the value to be updated.

Let's look at how we can make a CountFromNumber component that takes an initial value and then counts up from it, also updating the parent value:

```
Vue.component('count-from-number', {
  template: '<p>The number is {{ number }}</p>',
  props: {
    number: {
      type: Number,
      required: true
    }
  },
  mounted() {
    setInterval(() => {
      this.$emit('update:number', this.number + 1);
    }, 1000);
  }
});
```

The local value isn't being changed at all, but the component is changing the parent value that is being passed back down to the component.

In some cases, it might be beneficial to wrap the emit logic in a computed property, like so:

```
Vue.component('count-from-number', {
  template: '<p>The number is {{ localNumber }}</p>',
  props: {
    number: {
      type: Number,
      required: true
    }
  },
  computed: {
    localNumber: {
      get() {
        return this.number;
      },
      set(value) {
        this.$emit('update:number', value);
      }
    }
  },
```

```
  mounted() {
    setInterval(() => {
      this.localNumber++;
    }, 1000);
  }
});
```

Now, `localNumber` is effectively the same as `number`. It gets the value from the prop, and when it is updated, it emits the event to update the value in the parent component (where it will then be passed back down again as the updated value).

 Be careful of infinite loops when you're doing this: if both the parent and child components are reacting to changes and changing the value again, it will break your app!

If you just want to update the value passed in as a prop and don't care about updating the value on the parent component, you can copy the value from the prop into the data object by referring to `this` in the initial data function, like so:

```
Vue.component('count-from-number', {
  template: '<p>The number is {{ number }}</p>',
  props: {
    initialNumber: {
      type: Number,
      required: true
    }
  },
  data() {
    return {
      number: this.initialNumber
    };
  },
  mounted() {
    setInterval(() => {
      this.number++;
    }, 1000);
  }
}),
```

Note that if you do this, the component won't update when the prop value updates, because it will be referring to a different value. If you want to restart the counter from the new number provided, add a watcher for `initialNumber` that will copy the new value across to `number`.

Custom Inputs and v-model

Similarly to the .sync operator, it's possible to use v-model on your components in order to create custom inputs. Once again, it's syntactical sugar. Look at the following code:

```
<input-username
  v-model="username"
/>
```

That code is the equivalent of this:

```
<input-username
  :value="username"
  @input="value => username = value"
/>
```

So, to create our InputUsername component, we need it to do two things: first, it needs to read the initial value from the value prop, and then it needs to emit an input event whenever the value is changed. For the sake of this example, let's also make the component lowercase the values before it emits them.

We can't use either of the approaches (emitting the event in order to change the value or using a computed property) that worked in the previous section. Instead, we have to listen to the input event on the input:

```
Vue.component('input-username', {
  template: `<input type="text" :value="value" @input="handleInput">`,
  props: {
    value: {
      type: String,
      required: true
    }
  },
  methods: {
    handleInput(e) {
      const value = e.target.value.toLowerCase();

      // If value was changed, update it on the input too
      if (value !== e.target.value) {
        e.target.value = value;
      }

      this.$emit('input', value);
    }
  }
});
```

Now you can use this component just as you would an input element: using v-model will behave the same. The only difference is that you can't use capital letters!

The preceding example has a problem: if you type an uppercase letter, the cursor will be moved to the end of the string. This is fine when someone is entering a username for the first time, but if they're going back to change it, their cursor will seem to jump about.

It's an easy enough problem to solve, but beyond the scope of the previous example; before setting e.target.value, store the current cursor position, and set it again after you've made the change.

Passing Content into Components with Slots

In addition to passing data into components as props, Vue lets you pass HTML into them too. For example, let's say you want to create a custom button element. You could use an attribute to set the text:

```
<custom-button text="Press me!"></custom-button>
```

That would work, but it's much more natural like this:

```
<custom-button>Press me!</custom-button>
```

To use this content inside the component, you can use the <slot> tag as follows:

```
Vue.component('custom-button', {
  template: '<button class="custom-button"><slot></slot></button>'
});
```

Then, the following HTML will be generated:

```
<button class="custom-button">Press me!</button>
```

In addition to passing in strings, you can pass in any HTML you like; you can even pass in other Vue components. This allows you to create complicated documents without any of your components getting too big. For example, you could divide your page into a header component, a sidebar component, and a content component and write your template something like this:

```
<div class="app">
  <site-header></site-header>

  <div class="container">
    <site-sidebar>
      ...sidebar content goes here...
    </site-sidebar>

    <site-main>
      ...main content goes here...
    </site-main>
  </div>
</div>
```

This is a nice way of structuring sites, especially after you start using scoped CSS and vue-router, which are introduced later in the book.

Fallback Content

If you specify content inside the `<slot>` element, it will be used as fallback content when content isn't passed to the component. Let's give our `<custom-button>` component seen previously some default text as a fallback component:

```
Vue.component('custom-button', {
  template: `<button class="custom-button">
    <slot><span class="default-text">Default button text</span></slot>
  </button>`
});
```

Writing HTML inside the template string is getting unwieldy, so let's see that example again, but in an HTML block:

```
<button class="custom-button">
  <slot>
    <span class="default-text">Default button text</span>
  </slot>
</button>
```

You can see that in addition to having default text, the text is also wrapped in a span element with the `default-text` class. This is completely optional—you don't have to have a tag surrounding the content in a slot component or in the fallback content; you can use any HTML you want.

I cover how to separate your HTML from the component object in "vue-loader and .vue Files" on page 61. Using the template attribute works in only very simple examples.

Named Slots

In the previous section, you saw *single slots*. They're probably the most commonly used kind of slots and are certainly the simplest to understand: content passed to the component is output as the `<slot>` component inside the element.

There are also named slots. *Named slots* have—you guessed it—a name, which allows you to have multiple slots in the same component.

Let's say we have a simple blog post component with a header (usually a title, but maybe sometimes other things) and some text. The component could have the following template:

```
<section class="blog-post">
  <header>
    <slot name="header"></slot>
    <p>Post by {{ author.name }}</p>
```

```
    </header>

    <main>
      <slot></slot>
    </main>
  </section>
```

Then when we call the component in our template, we can use the `slot` attribute to say that a given element should be used as the header slot. The rest of the HTML will be used as the unnamed slot:

```
<blog-post :author="author">
  <h2 slot="header">Blog post title</h2>

  <p>Blog post content</p>

  <p>More blog post content</p>
</blog-post>
```

The generated HTML looks like the following:

```
<section class="blog-post">
  <header>
    <h2>Blog post title</h2>
    <p>Post by Callum Macrae</p>
  </header>

  <main>
    <p>Blog post content</p>

    <p>More blog post content</p>
  </main>
</section>
```

Scoped Slots

It's possible to pass data back into our slot components so that we can access component data in the parent component's markup.

Let's make a component that gets user information, but leaves the display of it to the parent element:

```
Vue.component('user-data', {
  template: '<div class="user"><slot :user="user"></slot></div>',
  data: () => ({
    user: undefined,
  }),
  mounted() {
    // Set this.user...
  }
});
```

Any properties passed to `<slot>` will be available on a variable defined in the `slot-scope` property. Let's call this component and display the user information with our own HTML:

```
<div>
  <user-data slot-scope="user">
    <p v-if="user">User name: {{ user.name }}</p>
  </user-data>
</div>
```

This functionality combined with named slots can be useful for overriding the styling of an element. Let's take a component that displays a list of blog post summaries:

```
<div>
  <div v-for="post in posts">
    <h1>{{ post.title }}</h1>
    <p>{{ post.summary }}</p>
  </div>
</div>
```

Pretty simple. It takes an array of posts as `posts`, and then outputs all the post titles and summaries. To use it, we can do this:

```
<blog-listing :posts="posts"></blog-listing>
```

Let's create a version of this in which we can pass in our own HTML to display the post summary—maybe, for example, on one page we want to display images instead. We need to wrap the paragraph element for the summary in a named slot element, which we can then override if we choose to.

Our new component looks like this:

```
<div>
  <div v-for="post in posts">
    <h1>{{ post.title }}</h1>

    <slot name="summary" :post="post">
      <p>{{ post.summary }}</p>
    </slot>
  </div>
</div>
```

Now, the original way we used the component still works fine, because the paragraph element is still available as a fallback if no slot element is provided, but if we choose to, we can override the post summary element.

Let's override the summary to display an image instead of the post summary:

```
<blog-listing :posts="posts">
  <img
    slot="summary"
    slot-scope="post"
    :src="post.image"
```

```
      :alt="post.summary">
</blog-listing>
```

Now the image element is used instead of the text element. We provided the post summary as the alternate text for the image, though; this is important so that users using assistive technology such as screen readers still know what the blog post is about.

Slot scope destructuring

As a neat shortcut, you can treat the slot-scope argument as if it were a function argument, so you can use destructuring.

Let's rewrite the previous example to use destructuring:

```
<blog-listing :posts="posts">
  <img
    slot="summary"
    slot-scope="{ image, summary }"
    :src="image"
    :alt="summary">
</blog-listing>
```

Custom Events

In addition to working with native DOM events, v-on works with custom events that you can emit from your components. To fire a custom event, use the this.$emit() method with the name of the event and any arguments you want to pass. Then you can use v-on on the component to listen to the event.

The following is a simple component that emits an event called count every time it is clicked:

```
<div id="app">
  <button @click="handleClick">Clicked {{ clicks }} times</button>
</div>

<script>
  new Vue({
    el: '#app',
    data: () => ({
      clicks: 0
    }),
    methods: {
      handleClick() {
        this.clicks++;
        this.$emit('count', this.clicks);
      }
    }
```

```
  });
  </script>
```

Every time the button is clicked, it fires the `count` event, and as an argument, the number of times the button has been clicked.

Then when we use the component, we can use `v-on` with the custom event just as we used `v-on` before with the click event to listen to the event. The following example takes the number that the counter emits and displays it to the page:

```
<div id="app">
  <counter v-on:count="handleCount"></counter>

  <p>clicks = {{ clicks }}</p>
</div>
<script>
  const Counter = {
    // component here
  };

  new Vue({
    el: '#app',
    data: {
      clicks: 0,
    },
    methods: {
      handleCount(clicks) {
        this.clicks = clicks;
      }
    },
    components: {
      Counter
    }
  });
</script>
```

When working inside a component, we can also listen to events that are being dispatched by that same component by using the $on method. It works pretty much the same as any event dispatcher: when you fire an event by using $emit, your event handler that was added using $on is triggered. You can't use this.$on to listen to events fired by child components; either use v-on on the component or use a ref on the component to call .$on on the component itself:

```
<div id="app">
  <counter ref="counter"></counter>
</div>
<script>
  // Incomplete component for brevity
  new Vue({
    el: '#app',
    mounted() {
```

```
        this.$refs.counter.$on('count', this.handleCount);
    }
  });
</script>
```

There are also two more methods for working with events: $once and $off. $once behaves the same as $on, but is fired only once—the first time the event is fired—and $off is used to remove an event listener. Both methods behave similarly to your standard event emitters such as EventEmitter in Node.js and the .on(), .once(), .off(), and .trigger() methods in jQuery.

Because Vue has a full event emitter built in, when you're using Vue, there is no need to import your own event emitter. Even when you're writing code as part of a Vue component, you can still take advantage of the Vue event emitter by creating a new instance using new Vue(). See the following example:

```
const events = new Vue();

let count = 0;
function logCount() {
  count++;
  console.log(`Debugger function called ${count} times`);
}

events.$on('test-event', logCount);

setInterval(() => {
  events.$emit('test-event');
}, 1000);

setTimeout(() => {
  events.$off('test-event');
}, 10000);
```

This code logs to the console once a second for 10 seconds until the event handler is removed by .$off().

This is especially useful for getting your Vue code to communicate with your non-Vue code—although it's generally better to use vuex instead if it's available.

Mixins

Mixins are a way of storing code to be reused across multiple elements. For example, let's say you have numerous components for displaying different types of users. Although most of what you want to display will depend on the type of user, a fair chunk of the logic will be common between the components. You can take three approaches here: you can have duplicate code across all the components (obviously not a good idea); you can take the common code, split it into functions, and store it in a util file; or you can use a mixin. The last two approaches are fairly similar in this example, but using a mixin is the more Vue way to do it—and in a lot of other examples that we'll be covering in this section, can be a lot more powerful.

Anything stored on the mixin will also be available on the component that the mixin is added to. Let's create a mixin that adds a method called getUserInformation() to the components it is added to:

```
const userMixin = {
  methods: {
    getUserInformation(userId) {
      return fetch(`/api/user/${userId}`)
        .then((res) => res.json);
    }
  }
};
```

Now you can add it in a component and use it like this:

```
import userMixin from './mixins/user';

Vue.component('user-admin', {
  mixins: [userMixin],
  template: '<div v-if="user">Name: {{ user.name }}</div>',
  props: {
    userId: {
      type: Number
    }
  }
  data: () => ({
    user: undefined
  }),
  mounted() {
    this.getUserInformation(this.userId)
      .then((user) => {
        this.user = user;
      });
  }
});
```

Vue will automatically have added the method to the component—it has been "mixed" in.

In addition to methods, mixins are able to access pretty much anything the Vue component can, as if it were part of the component itself. For example, let's change the mixin so that it is responsible for the storage of the data and the mounted hook:

```
const userMixin = {
  data: () => ({
    user: undefined
  }),
  mounted() {
    fetch(`/api/user/${this.userId}`)
      .then((res) => res.json())
```

```
      .then((user) => {
        this.user = user;
      });
    }
  }
```

Now the component can be simplified to this:

```
import userMixin from './mixins/user';

Vue.component('user-admin', {
  mixins: [userMixin],
  template: '<div v-if="user">Name: {{ name.user }}</div>',
  props: {
    userId: {
      type: Number
    }
  }
});
```

Although the component has been made a lot simpler, knowing where the data is coming from could become confusing. You need to consider this trade-off when deciding what to put in your mixins and what to put in your components.

Merging Mixins and Components

If a mixin and a component have duplicate keys—for example, if they both have a method called addUser() or they both use the created() hook—Vue handles them differently, depending on what they are.

For life-cycle hooks—for example, created() or beforeMount()—Vue adds them to an array and runs both of them:

```
const loggingMixin = {
  created() {
    console.log('Logged from mixin');
  }
};

Vue.component('example-component', {
  mixins: [loggingMixin],
  created() {
    console.log('Logged from component');
  }
});
```

When that component is created, both "Logged from mixin" and "Logged from component" will be logged to the console.

For duplicate methods, computed properties, or anything else that isn't a life-cycle hook, the property from the component will override the property from the mixin.

For example:

```
const loggingMixin2 = {
  methods: {
    log() {
      console.log('Logged from mixin');
    }
  }
};

Vue.component('example-component' {
  mixins: [loggingMixin2],
  created() {
    this.log();
  },
  methods: {
    log() {
      console.log('Logged from component');
    }
  }
};
```

Now when the console is created, only "Logged from component" is logged, as the log() method from the component has overridden the log() method from the mixin.

Sometimes this behavior might be intentional, but sometimes you might have accidentally named two methods in different places the same thing, which could lead to issues if one of them is overridden! For this reason, the official Vue Style Guide recommends that for private properties in mixins (methods, data, and computed properties that aren't supposed to be used outside the mixin), you should prefix their names with $yourMixinName. The log() method in the previous mixin would become $_loggingMixin2_log(). This is especially important when writing plug-ins, as users will be adding your plug-in to their own code.

vue-loader and .vue Files

In "Installation and Setup" on page 3, I discussed how to install Vue, and briefly covered how to set up vue-loader. Writing components by using Vue.component() or storing them as objects can be a bit messy, and with more complicated components, you don't really want to be writing a ton of HTML in the template property of the component. vue-loader adds a way to write one component per file in a logical and easy-to-understand syntax in .vue files.

If you've set up vue-loader, you can take this component you saw previously:

```
Vue.component('display-number', {
  template: '<p>The number is {{ number }}</p>',
  props: {
```

```
      number: {
        type: Number,
        required: true
      }
    }
  });
```

And turn it into this:

```
<template>
  <p>The number is {{ number }}</p>
</template>

<script>
  export default {
    props: {
      number: {
        type: Number,
        required: true
      }
    }
  };
</script>
```

If you save that as *display-number.vue*, you can then import it into your application and use it as if you had defined it by using the object syntax:

```
<div id="app">
  <display-number :number="4"></display-number>
</div>
<script>
  import DisplayNumber from './components/display-number.vue';

  new Vue({
    el: '#app',
    components: {
      DisplayNumber
    }
  });
</script>
```

After being processed by webpack and vue-loader, that code will work just like the previous example with the display-number component. It won't work at all in the browser; you need to use a preprocessor for this.

Splitting your components into files makes your code a lot easier to manage. Instead of having one large file with all your components, you can store them in files in relevantly named directories—perhaps named by the section of the site they're used on, or by the type or size of the component.

Non-prop Attributes

If you specify an attribute on a component that isn't used a prop, it's added to the root HTML element of the component. For instance, let's say we want to add a class to the `<display-number>` component in the previous example. You can add it to the location where you call the component:

```
<display-number class="some-class" :number="4"></display-number>
```

The following is the output:

```
<p class="some-class">The number is 4</p>
```

This works with any HTML property or attribute, not just `class`.

What happens if we specify the same attribute on both the component and root element of the component? Most of the time, if we specify the same attribute in both places, the attribute on the component will overwrite the attribute specified in the component template. For example, let's take the following code example:

```
<div id="app">
  <custom-button type="submit">Click me!</custom-button>
</div>
<script>
  const CustomButton = {
    template: '<button type="button"><slot></slot></button>'
  };

  new Vue({
    el: '#app',
    components: {
      CustomButton
    }
  });
</script>
```

In our component template, we're giving the button `type="button"`, but then when we call the component, we're specifying `type="submit"`. The attribute specified on the component, not inside the component, would override the other one, and the following would be output:

```
<button type="submit">Click me!</button>
```

Most attributes will overwrite the attribute inside the template, but `class` and `style` are slightly smarter, and their values will be merged. Let's take the following example:

```
<div id="app">
  <custom-button
    class="margin-top"
    style="font-weight: bold; background-color: red">
    Click me!
  </custom-button>
```

```
    </div>
    <script>
      const CustomButton = {
        template: `
          <button
            class="custom-button"
            style="color: yellow; background-color: blue">
            <slot></slot>
          </button>`
      };

      new Vue({
        el: '#app',
        components: {
          CustomButton
        }
      });
    </script>
```

The classes will be merged together to give custom-button margin-top, and the style attributes will be merged together to become color: yellow; background-color: red; font-weight: bold;. Note that the background-color from the component attribute has overridden the background-color from the component's template.

Components and v-for

When using v-for to loop through an array or object, and the array or object given to the directive changes, Vue doesn't regenerate every element again; it intelligently works out which elements need to change and changes only those ones. For example, if you have an array that is being output to the page as list elements and you add another item to the end of the list, the existing elements will be left alone, and a new element will be created at the end. If an item in the middle of the array is changed, only the corresponding element is changed.

If, however, you remove or add an item in the middle of the list, Vue won't calculate which is the corresponding element for the item removed; it will update every single element from that point to the end of the list, where it will add or remove a new element. With simple content, this probably isn't an issue, but with more complicated content and with components, you'll want to stop Vue from doing that.

Vue allows you to specify a key when using v-for so that you can tell Vue which element should be associated with each item of the array and the correct element is deleted. By default, the key is the index of the element within the loop. You can see how this behavior works by using the following code:

```
<template>
  <demo-key v-for="(item, i) in items" @click.native="items.splice(i, 1)">
    {{ item }}
```

```
    </demo-key>
</template>

<script>
  const randomColor = () => `hsl(${Math.floor(Math.random() * 360)}, 75%, 85%)`;

  const DemoKey = {
    template: `<p :style="{ backgroundColor: color }"><slot></slot></p>`,
    data: () => ({
      color: randomColor()
    })
  };

  export default {
    data: () => ({
      items: ['one', 'two', 'three', 'four', 'five']
    }),
    components: {
      DemoKey
    }
  };
</script>
```

The click handler is added using the `.native` modifier, because that's how you can add event listeners for native DOM events to components. Without `.native`, the event handler wouldn't be called.

That outputs five randomly colored paragraph elements containing the numbers one through five, as follows:

one	Mint Green
two	Pink
three	Yellow
four	Rose
five	Blue

Clicking one of the paragraphs removes the corresponding item from the `items` array. If we click the second element—in the image, the element labeled *two*—you'd expect that that element would be completely removed, and the element containing *three* would become the second element. Not so! What you end up with is the following:

one	Mint Green
three	Pink
four	Yellow
five	Rose

This is because of the way Vue's diffing mechanism works: you removed the second item, so it updates the text of that element to reflect the change, and then the next element, and then the next element, and then the array has ended, so it removes the final element. That probably wasn't what you desired in this case, though, so let's add a key to the example so that Vue knows which element to delete:

```
<template>
  <demo-key
    v-for="(item, i) in items" :key="item"
    @click.native="items.splice(i, 1)">
    {{ item }}
  </demo-key>
</template>
```

The key should be a unique number or string that corresponds to the item in the array. In this case, the array items themselves are just strings, so we can use them as the keys.

 I've fairly frequently seen people specify the key to be the index of the array (for instance, :key="i" in the previous example). Except in some specific cases, you probably don't want to do that! Although it will stop the warnings, you'll run into exactly the same issue I just showed you, with a different element from what you'd expect being deleted.

Now, clicking the second element will remove *two* from the array, and the corresponding element, resulting in the following:

one	Mint Green
three	Yellow
four	Rose
five	Blue

In general, specify a key wherever you can. It's not optional when using `v-for` directly on a component, as you saw in the previous example. Vue will have logged warnings to the console in that example.

Summary

Components are great for separating your code into logical chunks, each of which can perform a specific task. In this chapter you learned how to create and use components, both globally with `Vue.component()` and locally using the `components` property and objects.

You also saw how to pass data into components by using props, how to validate those props, and how data flows down but not up unless you use `.sync`, or for inputs, custom `update` events.

I showed you how to use slots to pass other HTML and components into components, easily enabling you to make layout components and fallback content.

You looked at custom events, which you can use to send information from a component to its parent.

You also learned to use mixins to move common logic out of components and share it between multiple components.

You looked at vue-loader and how you can use it when using webpack to create single-file components—a file that contains a component and nicely separates the HTML, JavaScript, and styling logic.

Finally, you also learned what happens if you specify an attribute on a component that isn't used as a prop, and why you should use `:key` when using `v-for` on a component.

CHAPTER 3

Styling with Vue

Vue helps you style your website or application in a few ways. `v-bind:class` and `v-bind:style` both have special helpers to help you set the class attribute and inline styles from your data, and when you're using components with vue-loader, it's possible to write scoped CSS that will affect only the component that CSS is writing in.

Class Binding

It's common to use `v-bind` with the class attribute in order to add or remove classes depending on your data. Vue adds a couple of neat enhancements when using `v-bind` to set the class attribute, making it a lot nicer to work with.

If you've used the classNames utility in React, you'll be fairly familiar with the `v-bind` syntax. It's basically the same, except wrapped in an array instead of being arguments of a function.

If you pass an array to `v-bind:class`, the classes in the array will be joined together. This is great for times when you want to set classes from your data or computed properties. Take the following example:

```
<div id="app">
  <div v-bind:class="[firstClass, secondClass]">
    ...
  </div>
</div>
<script>
  new Vue({
    el: '#app',
    data: {
```

```
        firstClass: 'foo'
      },
      computed: {
        secondClass() {
          return 'bar';
        }
      }
    });
  </script>
```

In this example, firstClass equals foo and secondClass evaluates to bar, so the div element would be given a class attribute of foo bar.

In addition to using arrays, you can use objects. An object will conditionally add the keys as classes depending on the values: if the value is truthy, the key will be added as a class; otherwise, if it is false, it will not.

For example, if the bound class is { *my-class*: shouldAddClass }, the element will have the *my-class* element if shouldAddClass evaluates to a truthy value. You can also specify more than one class in the object. Take the following example:

```
<div id="app">
  <div v-bind:class="classes"></div>
</div>
<script>
  new Vue({
    el: '#app',
    data: {
      shouldBeBar: true
    },
    computed: {
      classes() {
        return {
          foo: true,
          bar: this.shouldBeBar,
          hello: false
        };
      }
    }
  });
</script>
```

Once again in this example, the generated class attribute will be foo bar: foo is set to true; bar is set to this.shouldBeBar, which evaluated to true; and hello is set to false, so isn't applied to the element.

Although I've returned the object from a computed property, this is entirely optional, and you can specify the object inline. It's just a nice pattern to avoid the line getting too long when you have more than a couple of classes.

It's also possible to mix both arrays and objects by using the objects inside an array when you want to add classes from both variables and conditionally add classes:

```
<div v-bind:class="[
    'my-class',
    classFromVariable,
    { 'conditional-class': hasClass }
]"></div>
```

You can, of course, specify the classes as a normal string or from a variable containing the class name if you don't need any of the functionality from using arrays or objects.

Inline Style Binding

Similar to v-bind:class, covered in the previous section, Vue also has a special helper for the style attribute. Instead of you having to concatenate strings to specify inline styles, you can specify them as an object instead:

```
<div v-bind:style="{ fontWeight: 'bold', color: 'red' }"></div>
```

Note that we're writing fontWeight, not 'font-weight'. Vue automatically converts the object's properties from camel case to their equivalent CSS properties, which means we don't have to worry about escaping them.

Although it's generally better to style elements by using classes when possible, inline style binding is useful for setting styles from variables. For example, the following example outputs 12 elements of different colors, creating a color swatch:

```
<div id="app">
  <div
    v-for="n in 12"
    class="color"
    :style="{ backgroundColor: getColor(n) }">
  </div>
</div>
<script>
  new Vue({
    el: '#app',
    methods: {
      getColor(n) {
        return `hsl(${(n - 1) * 30}, 100%, 75%)`;
      }
    }
  });
</script>
```

After applying some CSS, we can see a colour swatch: a red box, followed by an orange box, all the way through to pink.

Vue also handles vendor prefixing for you automatically: if you set a style that requires a vendor prefix, Vue will automatically add that for you.

Array Syntax

You can use an array to specify multiple style objects:

```
<div :style="[baseStyles, moreStyles]">...</div>
```

The styles from both objects will be applied, with the styles from moreStyles overriding baseStyles if both specify the same styles.

Multiple Values

It's also possible to provide multiple values in an array to set the last value that the browser supports:

```
<div :style="{ display: ['-webkit-box', '-ms-flexbox', 'flex'] }">...</div>
```

That'll set display: flex if it is supported; otherwise, it'll attempt -ms-flexbox, and otherwise, -webkit-box.

Scoped CSS with vue-loader

You previously saw how to use vue-loader to split your components into individual *.vue* files. As a quick reminder, here's an example from "vue-loader and .vue Files" on page 61:

```
<template>
  <p>The number is {{ number }}</p>
</template>

<script>
  export default {
    props: {
      number: {
        type: Number,
        required: true
      }
    }
  };
</script>
```

In addition to the <template> and <script> tags, it's also possible to put <style> tags in these files, which will then be output onto the page (or you can set up webpack to extract it into an external CSS file). Let's say we want to style the previous example so that the number is bold:

```
<template>
  <p>The number is <span class="number">{{ number }}</span></p>
</template>

<script>
  export default {
```

```
    props: {
      number: {
        type: Number,
        required: true
      }
    }
  };
</script>

<style>
  .number {
    font-weight: bold;
  }
</style>
```

The number is now bold.

Unlike the JavaScript, the CSS in that component will affect all the HTML on the page, not just the component. Vue has a way to fix this: scoped CSS. If we add the scoped attribute to the style tag, Vue will automatically process the CSS and HTML so that the CSS affects only the HTML in that component.

Let's take a look at how it works. If we add the scoped attribute to the previous style tag (so that it is now <style scoped>), the following HTML is output:

```
<p data-v-e0e8ddca>The number is <span data-v-e0e8ddca class="number">10
  </span></p>

<style>
.number[data-v-e0e8ddca] {
  font-weight: bold;
}
</style>
```

You can see that Vue has added a data attribute to every element that's part of the component, and then added it to the CSS selector so that the CSS is applied to only those elements.

CSS Modules with vue-loader

As an alternative to scoped CSS, you can use CSS modules with vue-loader:

```
<template>
  <p>The number is <span :class="$style.number">{{ number }}</span></p>
</template>

<style module>
  .number {
    font-weight: bold;
  }
</style>
```

The .number style will be replaced by a random style name, and $style.number will evaluate to that name, so the CSS specified in the .number selector will be applied to only that single element.

Preprocessors

You can configure vue-loader to run your CSS, JavaScript, and HTML through pre-processors. Say you want to write SCSS instead of CSS to take advantage of features such as nesting and variables. You can do that in two steps—first, install sass-loader and node-sass using npm, and then add lang="scss" to your style tag:

```
<style lang="scss" scoped>
  $color: red;

  .number {
    font-weight: bold;
    color: $color;
  }
</style>
```

It's as simple as that. Scoped CSS is still handled automatically; there are no extra steps to get it working again.

vue-loader has a load of other features that are beyond the scope of this book. If you're going to use it, I'd definitely recommend giving the documentation a read.

A lot of these features are also available in vueify, the Browserify equivalent of vue-loader. However, vueify is not as popular as vue-loader, so I don't cover it here.

Summary

In this short chapter, you looked at various ways Vue helps you style your application. You looked at the special v-bind:class and v-bind:style attributes, which make it easier to add and set classes and styles. You also learned about a few styling-specific features of vue-loader: scoped CSS, CSS modules, and preprocessing.

CHAPTER 4

Render Functions and JSX

You've already seen how to use the template attribute to set the HTML of a component, and you've also seen how to use vue-loader to write your component HTML in a <template> tag. However, using templates isn't the only way to indicate what Vue should display on the page: you can choose to use a render function instead. This also enables you to write JSX in your Vue application, which if you're from a React background, you may be more comfortable with (although I still recommend giving templates a try!).

You can also use the template attribute in your main Vue instance instead of having Vue use the HTML in your Vue element. It'll be automatically added to the element you specify as the Vue element.

When you pass a function to the render property of your Vue instance, the function is passed a createElement function, which you can use to indicate the HTML that should be output to the page. As a simple example, the following renders <h1>Hello world!</h1> to the page:

```
new Vue({
  el: '#app',
  render(createElement) {
    return createElement('h1', 'Hello world!');
  }
});
```

createElement takes three arguments: the tag name of the element to be generated, an object containing options (such as HTML attributes, properties, event listeners, and class and style bindings), and either a child node or an array of child nodes. The tag name is required, and the other two are optional (and if you don't specify the attributes object, you can specify the children as the second argument). Let's look at each of those individually.

The Tag Name

The tag name is the simplest argument and the only required one. It can be either a string, or a function that returns a string. In the previous example, we're returning h1, so an `<h1>` element will be created. Render functions also have access to this, so you can set the tag name from a property of the data object, prop, computed property, or anything like that:

```
new Vue({
  el: '#app',
  render(createElement) {
    return createElement(this.tagName, 'Hello world');
  },
  data: {
    tagName: 'h1'
  }
});
```

This capability is a big advantage of render functions over templates, in which it isn't easy or readable to set a tag name dynamically. `<{{ tagName }}>` is invalid (and still not that easy to read!).

The Data Object

The data object is where you specify attributes that will affect the component or element. If you were writing a template, that's everything that goes between the tag name and the closing >. For example, with `<custom-button type="submit" v-bind:text="buttonText">`, the attributes would be `type="submit"` `v-bind:text="buttonText"`.

In this example, `type` is a normal HTML attribute being passed through to the component, and `text` is a component prop bound to the `buttonText` variable. For the same example using `createElement`, you could write the following:

```
new Vue({
  el: '#app',
  render(createElement) {
    return createElement('custom-button', {
      attrs: {
        type: 'submit'
      },
      props: {
        text: this.buttonText
      }
    });
```

```
    }
  });
```

You'll notice that we're not using v-bind at all anymore; this is because we can refer to the variable directly as this.buttonText. Because this.buttonText is a dependency of the function, the render function will be called again whenever buttonText is updated and the DOM updated automatically, the same as with templates.

See Example 4-1 for all the options required to do everything you've learned so far in this book.

Example 4-1. The attributes of the options object

```
{
  // HTML attributes
  attrs: {
    type: 'submit'
  },

  // Props to be passed to components
  props: {
    text: 'Click me!'
  },

  // DOM properties such as innerHTML (instead of v-html)
  domProps: {
    innerHTML: 'Some HTML'
  },

  // Event listeners
  on: {
    click: this.handleClick
  },

  // The same as slot="exampleSlot" - used when the component is a child of
  // another component
  slot: 'exampleSlot',

  // The same as key="exampleKey" - used for components generated in a loop
  key: 'exampleKey',

  // The same as ref="exampleRef"
  ref: 'exampleRef',

  // The same as v-bind:class="['example-class'...
  class: ['example-class', { 'conditional-class': true }],

  // The same as v-bind:style="{ backgroundColor: 'red' }"
  style: { backgroundColor: 'red' }
}
```

Note that `class` and `style` are specified separately from the `attrs` property. This is because of the `v-bind` helpers; if you just specify the class or styles as a property of the `attrs` object, you won't be able to specify classes as an array or object, or your styles as an object.

There are a couple of other properties for things that haven't been covered in this book: check out the official documentation for a full list.

Children

The third and final argument is where you specify the children of the element. This can either be an array or a string. If it's a string, the specified string will be rendered as the text of the element; and if it's an array, you can call `createElement` again inside the array to generate a complicated tree.

 If you're specifying children but not the data object, you can pass this as the second argument instead of the third.

Let's take the following template from a previous section:

```
<div>
  <button v-on:click="counter++">Click to increase counter</button>
  <p>You've clicked the button {{ counter }}</p> times.
</div>
```

To write the same template by using `createElement`, you'd write the following:

```
render(createElement) {
  return createElement(
    'div',
    [
      createElement(
        'button',
        {
          on: {
            click: () => this.counter++,
          }
        },
        'Click to increase counter'
      ),
      createElement(
        'p',
        `You've clicked the button ${this.counter} times`
      )
    ]
```

```
    );
  }
```

JSX

The previous example seems like a lot of code to do what we did in a four-line template. Luckily, with the help of *babel-plugin-transform-vue-jsx*, you can write your `ren der` function by using JSX along with the Babel plug-in to compile the JSX into `createElement` calls that Vue understands. Note that internally (and throughout the JSX ecosystem), the `createElement` function is usually aliased to a shorter name, `h`, but you don't normally need to know that.

I won't cover how to install *babel-plugin-transform-vue-jsx* here; check out the documentation for the plug-in to see how to do that.

After the Babel plug-in has been installed, the previous code can be rewritten like so:

```
render() {
  return (
    <div>
      <button onClick={this.clickHandler}>Click to increase counter</button>
      <p>You've clicked the button {counter} times</p>
    </div>
  );
}
```

That's much better. A couple of other nice features of JSX work with Vue too.

In addition to being able to import and use components the same way you can in templates—by specifying the name of the component as the tag name—it's also possible to import components the React way too. If the variable the component is imported with begins with a capital letter, you can use it without having to put it in the `components` object or using `Vue.component()`. For example:

```
import MyComponent from './components/MyComponent.vue';

new Vue({
  el: '#app',
  render() {
    return (
      <MyComponent />
    );
  }
});
```

JSX spread is also supported. Just as with React, you can use the spread operator on an object of properties, and it will be merged with the other properties you've specified and applied to the element:

```
render() {
  const props = {
    class: 'world',
    href: 'https://www.oreilly.com/'
  };

  return (
    <a class="hello" {...props}>O'Reilly Media</a>
  );
}
```

This would generate a link to *oreilly.com* (*https://www.oreilly.com*) with a class attribute equal to `hello world`.

Summary

This chapter explained how you can use render functions as an alternative to template strings to build HTML. You do this by using the `createElement` function, which takes three arguments: the tag name, the data object, and the children of the element. You can also use JSX instead of calling `createElement`, using *babel-plugin-transform-vue-jsx*.

CHAPTER 5

Client-Side Routing with vue-router

With the core Vue.js library introduced in the previous chapters, we can display and work with data on a page. However, a fully featured website requires more than just that. You may have noticed on some websites that you can navigate around the site without downloading the new page from the server, or if you've used another framework before, you've probably already met client-side routing.

vue-router is a library for Vue that means we can handle the routing of an app in the browser instead of on the server as in traditional websites. Routing is the act of taking a path (for example, */users/12345/posts*) and deciding what should be displayed on the page.

Installation

As with Vue itself, there are multiple ways to install vue-router. You can use a CDN by adding the following:

```
<script src="https://unpkg.com/vue-router"></script>
```

Or if you're using npm, you can install it using `npm install --save vue-router`. Then, if you're using a bundler such as webpack, you will need to call `Vue.use(VueRouter)` to install vue-router:

```
import Vue from 'vue';
import VueRouter from 'vue-router';

Vue.use(VueRouter);
```

This step adds components to your app that you will meet in the next few sections.

Basic Usage

To set up the router, you need to give it an array of paths and the corresponding components: when the path is matched, the component will be displayed.

The following creates a simple two-path router:

```
import PageHome from './components/pages/Home';
import PageAbout from './components/pages/About';

const router = new VueRouter({
  routes: [
    {
      path: '/',
      component: PageHome
    },
    {
      path: '/about',
      component: PageAbout
    }
  ]
});
```

Now to use that router, we have to do two things. First, we have to pass it in to Vue when we initialize our application. Then, to get it to display on the page, we need to add a special `<router-view />` component.

To pass the router into Vue, you can just pass it in using the `router` property when you initialize Vue:

```
import router from './router';

new Vue({
  el: '#app',
  router: router
});
```

Then in your template, put the `<router-view />` component wherever you want the component returned by the router to display.

See Example 5-1 for a full basic setup that will display different things depending on the path requested.

Example 5-1. Sample code of a router using vue-router

```
<div id="app">
  <h1>Site title</h1>

  <main>
    <router-view />
  </main>
```

```
  <p>Page footer</p>
</div>
<script>
  const PageHome = {
    template: '<p>This is the home page</p>'
  };
  const PageAbout = {
    template: '<p>This is the about page</p>'
  };

  const router = new VueRouter({
    routes: [
      { path: '/', component: PageHome },
      { path: '/about', component: PageAbout }
    ]
  });

  new Vue({
    el: '#app',
    router,
  });
</script>
```

After setting up the router and adding styling, you will see the following content when you access the root path:

Page title

This is the home page

Page footer

And you'll see the following when you access /about:

Page title

This is the about page

Page footer

HTML5 History Mode

By default, vue-router uses the URL hash to store the path. To access the *about* route on *<yoursite>.com*, you would go to *http://<yoursite>.com/#/about*. However, nearly every browser these days supports the HTML5 history API, which allows developers to update the URL without going to a new page.

You can tell vue-router to use the HTML5 history API by changing the router mode to history:

```
const router = new VueRouter({
  mode: 'history',
  routes: [
    { path: '/', component: PageHome },
    { path: '/about', component: PageAbout }
  ]
});
```

Now, if you go to *http://<yoursite>.com/about*, you get...a 404 page. In addition to telling the client-side code to look at the full path instead of the hash, you need to tell your server to respond with your HTML page on every request it doesn't recognize (for example, not when you request a CSS file).[1]

The way you do this varies, depending on what's powering your server, but it's generally pretty simple—the vue-router documentation has a section for most popular servers.

---

1 Many static site hosts have an SPA mode that you can enable to do this. Check that out before worrying about server configuration.

Dynamic Routing

The previous example is great for simple sites, but what if we want to do something more complicated, such as match a user ID as part of a path? vue-router supports dynamic path matching, meaning that you can specify the path by using a special syntax, and the component will be accessible under all the paths that match that route. For example, if we wanted to have our component display when the path is */user/1234*, where *1234* can be anything, we can specify the following route:

```
const router = new VueRouter({
  routes: [
    {
      path: '/user/:userId',
      component: PageUser
    }
  ]
});
```

Then any path matching */user/:userId* will be shown the `PageUser` component.

vue-router uses the path-to-regexp library for this—the same library used by Express, Koa (both the official and unofficial routers), and react-router, so if you've used any of those before, you will recognize this syntax.

Inside the component, you can access the current route by using the `this.$route` property. This object contains useful properties such as the full path currently being accessed, the query parameters of the URL (for example, `?lang=en`), and most usefully for this example, a `params` object containing all the parts of the URL that were matched dynamically. With this example, if you access */user/1234*, the `params` object will equal the following:

```
{
  "userId": "1234"
}
```

You can then use this data to do whatever you want with. In this case, you might want to use it to send off an API request to grab the users, data, and then display it on the page.

Although you might expect that `userId` would be a number, vue-router has extracted it from a path (which is a string) and has no way of knowing that it is supposed to be a number, so `userId` is in fact a string. If you want to use it as a number, you'll have to convert it yourself by using `parseInt`, `parseFloat`, or `Number`.

Note that the dynamic part of the URL doesn't have to be at the end of the URL: */user/1234/posts* is perfectly valid. Also, you can have more than one dynamic segment: matching */user/1234/posts/2* against */user/:userId/posts/:pageNumber* will result in the following params object:

```
{
  "userId": "1234",
  "pageNumber": "2"
}
```

Reacting to Route Updates

When navigating between */user/1234* and */user/5678*, the same component will be reused, and so none of the life-cycle hooks covered in Chapter 1 such as mounted will be called. Instead, you can use the beforeRouteUpdate guard to run some code when the dynamic segment of the URL changes.

Let's create a PageUser component that calls an API when it is mounted, and calls it again when the route changes:

```
<template>
  <div v-if="state === 'loading'">
    Loading user…
  </div>
  <div>
    <h1>User: {{ userInfo.name }}</h1>
    ... etc ...
  </div>
</template>

<script>
  export default {
    data: () => ({
      state: 'loading',
      userInfo: undefined
    }),
    mounted() {
      this.init();
    },
    beforeRouteUpdate(to, from, next) {
      this.state = 'loading';
      this.init();
      next();
    },
    methods: {
      init() {
        fetch(`/api/user/${this.$route.params.userId}`)
          .then((res) => res.json())
          .then((data) => {
            this.userInfo = data;
          });
```

```
      }
    }
  };
</script>
```

The preceding code loads the data for the first user from the API, displays that information, and then if the route changes (say, if the user clicks a link to go from one user to another), it makes another call to the API to get the data for the second user.

Note that we've moved the logic that we would usually have in mounted into a method, which we call both in the mounted hook and the beforeRouteUpdate guard. This avoids having duplicate code—we pretty much always want to be doing the same thing in both places.

We'll explore guards further later in this chapter, including why you have to call next() at the end of the function.

 beforeRouteUpdate was added in Vue 2.2 and so wasn't available before then. Before 2.2, you had to watch the $route object for changes:

```
const PageUser = {
  template: '<div>...user page...</div>',
  watch: {
    '$route'() {
      console.log('Route updated');
    }
  }
};
```

Passing Params to Components as Props

As an alternative to using this.$route.params in your component, you can get vue-router to pass in the params as props to your router component. For example, let's take the following component:

```
const PageUser = {
  template: '<p>User ID: {{ $route.params.userId }}</p>'
};

const router = new VueRouter({
  routes: [
    {
      path: '/user/:userId',
      component: PageUser
    }
  ]
});
```

Navigating to *user/1234* will result in "User ID: 1234" being output to the page.

To tell vue-router to pass the user ID in as a prop instead, you can specify `props: true` on the router:

```
const PageUser = {
  props: ['userId'],
  template: '<p>User ID: {{ userId }}</p>'
};

const router = new VueRouter({
  routes: [
    {
      path: '/user/:userId',
      component: PageUser,
      props: true
    }
  ]
});
```

The advantage of using props instead of referring to `$route.params` is that the component is no longer closely coupled to vue-router. Imagine in the future you want to display more than one user per page; with the first code example, that would be tricky, but with the second example, it would be a lot easier, as you could just call the component in another page as if it were an ordinary component.

Nested Routes

You'll find that after you build sufficiently complicated apps, you'll have sections of your sites in which you want every page to have common styling or content. For example, maybe you have an admin section and you want to add another header below your normal site header to navigate around your admin section, or maybe you have a page displaying a product and you want to add a tab component that changes the URL too. For some examples, such as the admin section header example, it would be easy enough to just store the header in a component and manually include it on every single page. For other examples, such as a product page that has only a small portion of the content that is changing, you don't really want the individual tabs to be responsible for displaying the rest of the page—it's much better to use a nested route instead.

A *nested route* allows you to specify children of a route and gives you another `<router-view />` component to display them in. For example, let's build a settings section of a website, with a sidebar for navigating between settings pages. */settings/profile* will be a page for users to modify their profiles, and */settings/email* will allow them to modify their email preferences.

The profile page at *settings/profile* looks like this:

Site header

Profile

Email

This is the content for the profile settings page.

The email preferences page at *settings/email* looks like this:

Site header

Profile

Email

This is the content for the email settings page.

As you can see, both pages share a header and a sidebar. The header will be dealt with the normal way (it will be outside the root <router-view /> component), but we don't want the sidebar to display on all pages, only the settings pages.

To achieve this, we create a *settings* route, and then give that route two child routes, profile and email. Here is what the router looks like:

```
import PageSettings from './components/pages/Settings';
import PageSettingsProfile from './components/pages/SettingsProfile';
import PageSettingsEmail from './components/pages/SettingsEmail';

const router = new VueRouter({
  routes: [
    {
      path: '/settings',
      component: PageSettings,
      children: [
        {
```

```
            path: 'profile',
            component: PageSettingsProfile,
          },
          {
            path: 'email',
            component: PageSettingsEmail,
          }
        ]
      }
    ]
});
```

Then, in the `PageSettings` component, we can use another `<router-view />` component:

```
<div>
  <the-sidebar />
  <router-view />
</div>
```

Now, accessing *settings/profile* results in the following HTML:

```
<div id="app">
  <h1>Site title</h1>

  <main>
    <div>
      <div class="sidebar">
        ...sidebar HTML...
      </div>
    </div>

    <div class="page-profile">
      ...profile settings page HTML...
    </div>
  </main>

  <p>Page footer</p>
</div>
```

As you can see, the page has the header and footer from outside the root `<router-view />` from the example in the first section of this paragraph, the sidebar from inside the settings page but outside the second `<router-view />` component, and the contents of the profile settings page.

Redirect and Alias

Sometimes you want to redirect from one page to another; for example, maybe you've decided to rename *settings* to *preferences*. In that case, you don't want your users who are used to going to *settings* to see an error page, and you don't want search engines to be linking to pages that don't exist anymore.

To do this, you can specify a route with a `direct` property instead of a `component`:

```
const router = new VueRouter({
  routes: [
    {
      path: '/settings',
      redirect: '/preferences'
    }
  ]
});
```

Now, anyone accessing */settings* will be redirected to */preferences.*

An alternative to using redirects is to specify an alias of a component. For example, if you want the settings page to be accessible from both */settings* and */preferences*, you can give the `/settings` route an `alias` of `/preferences`:

```
import PageSettings from './components/pages/Settings';

const router = new VueRouter({
  routes: [
    {
      path: '/settings',
      alias: '/preferences',
      component: PageSettings
    }
  ]
});
```

I've found this useful in the past when I want both */user* and */user/:userId* to point to the same component.

Navigation

OK, so we have some routing now. If you navigate to */user/1234*, you will see a different thing than if you navigate to */preferences*, even though the same content is being served by the server. But how can we enable the user to navigate between routes? The obvious answer—using `<a>` tags—isn't the best one. Although using anchors to link between pages will technically work, if you're using HTML5 history mode, the page will reload every time you click a link, as in a traditional website. We can do better! Because everything is handled client-side, we can navigate between pages without having to reload the page. The router will even update the URL for you.

To do this, use the `<router-link>` element instead of the `<a>` element. It works similarly to the traditional anchor tag:

```
<router-link to="/user/1234">Go to user #1234</router-link>
```

Clicking that link will immediately take you to */user/1234* without having to load a new page. This improves the performance of your sites a ton. After the initial page load, it's super quick to navigate between pages as the HTML, JavaScript, and CSS has been downloaded already.

In addition to handling navigation without forcing the page to reload, vue-router also automatically handles your mode for you: using hash mode, the preceding link will take you to *#/user/1234*, whereas using history mode, it'll take you to */user/1234*.

The `<router-link>` component has a few properties beyond to. I cover the most important ones here, but check out the API documentation for the full list.

The output Tag

By default, using `<router-link>` results in an `<a>` tag being output to the page. For instance, the example from the previous section results in the following output:

```
<a href="/user/1234">Go to user #1234</a>
```

 The href won't be used if you click the link, as Vue will have added an event listener that will cancel the default click event to handle the navigation itself. It's still useful to have for a few reasons, though, such as being able to see where a link is going by hovering over it or being able to open a link in a new tab (which isn't handled by vue-router).

Sometimes, however, you might want to output an element other than an anchor tag, such as a list element in a navigation bar. You can use the `tag` property to do that:

```
<router-link to="/user/1234" tag="li">Go to user #1234</router-link>
```

This results in the following being output to the page:

```
<li>Go to user #1234</li>
```

Vue will then add an event listener to the element that detects when it is clicked and deals with the navigation.

This isn't optimal, though—as we've lost the anchor tag and the href attribute, we've lost a couple of important native browser behaviors: the browser doesn't know that the list item is a link, so hovering over it won't give you any information about the link; you can't right-click and open the link in a new tab; and assistive technology such as a screen reader won't announce the element as a link.

To fix this, we can add an anchor tag into the `<router-link>` element:

```
<router-link to="/user/1234" tag="li"><a>Go to user #1234</a></router-link>
```

The output HTML is now as follows:

```
<li><a href="/user/1234">Go to user #1234</a></li>
```

Perfect. vue-router will handle the routing when it can, but we'll have all the normal behavior we expect from links.

Active Class

A link is *active* when the path in the to property of the <router-link> component matches the path of the current page. If you're on */user/1234*, that link will be active.

When a link is active, vue-router automatically applies a class to the generated element. By default, this class is router-link-active, but you can configure the class added by using the active-class property. This is useful when you're using a UI library or existing code in which the active link is already set to something else. For example, if you're using Bootstrap and have a navigation bar (*navbar* in Bootstrap), you set the current active link by using the active class.

Let's get a simple Bootstrap navbar working with Vue. Here's what we're aiming for:

```
<ul class="nav navbar-nav">
  <li class="active"><a href="/blog">Blog</a></li>
  <li><a href="/user/1234">User #1234</a></li>
</ul>
```

We need to change two things. First, the active class is being added to the li element, not the a element, so we need to tell vue-router to output an li element instead of the default a link. Second, the class being added is active, not router-link-active, so that needs changing too.

Here's our Vue-ified code:

```
<ul class="nav navbar-nav">
  <router-link to="/blog" tag="li" active-class="active">
    <a>Blog</a>
  </router-link>
  <router-link to="/user/1234" tag="li" active-class="active">
    <a>User #1234</a>
  </router-link>
</ul>
```

The outputted HTML is exactly the same as the example before we added Vue; vue-router even adds the href attribute to the <a> elements.

Native Events

If you want to add a click event handler to a <router-link>, you can't just use @click. The following will not work:

```
<!-- This will not work -->
<router-link to="/blog" @click="handleClick">Blog</router-link>
```

By default, using `v-on` on a component listens to custom events emitted by the component. You saw this in Chapter 2. You can use the `.native` modifier to listen to the native event instead of the custom event:

```
<router-link to="/blog" @click.native="handleClick">Blog</router-link>
```

Now when the link is clicked, the `handleClick` method will be called.

Programmatic Navigation

In addition to enabling the user to navigate using links, you can also navigate programmatically using a couple of methods on the router. The methods imitate the browser's native history methods—`history.pushState()`, `history.replaceState()`, and `history.go()`—so if you're familiar with them, you'll recognize the syntax.

To go to a path, you can use `router.push()` (or `this.$router.push()` if you're in a component):

```
router.push('/user/1234');
```

This does the equivalent of clicking a `<router-link>` component with a `to` property of `/user/1234`—in fact, vue-router uses `router.push()` internally when you click a `<router-link>` component.

There's also `router.replace()`, which behaves similarly to `router.push()`: it'll take you to the route you've specified. The difference is that while `router.push()` will add a new entry to the history—so, if the user presses the Back button, the router will go back to the previous route—`router.replace()` replaces the current entry, so the Back button will go back to the route before.

Generally, you want `router.push()`, but `router.replace()` is useful in specific cases. For example, if you have human-readable article URLs such as */blog/hello-world*, if the user renames the post, you might want to use `router.replace()` to go to */blog/hello-world*, as there is no point in having both URLs in the history.

Finally, `router.go()` allows you to navigate backward and forward through history, as if pressing the browser Back and Forward buttons. To go back a record, you'd use `router.go(-1)`, and to go forward 10 records, you'd use `router.go(1)`. If there aren't that many records, the function call will fail silently.

Navigation Guards

Let's say you want to restrict users who aren't logged in from accessing certain sections of your app. You have a `userAuthenticated()` function that returns `true` if the user is logged in, but what now?

vue-router provides functionality that allows you to run code before navigation occurs and, if you tell it to, cancel the navigation or send the user somewhere else.

You can use `router.beforeEach()` to add a guard to the router. It's passed three arguments: `to`, `from`, and `next`, where `to` and `from` are the routes being navigated to and from, and `next` is a callback where you can tell vue-router to proceed with the navigation, cancel it, redirect to somewhere else, or register an error.

Let's look at a guard that stops unauthenticated users from being able to access anything starting with */account*:

```
router.beforeEach((to, from, next) => {
  if (to.path.startsWith('/account') && !userAuthenticated()) {
    next('/login');
  } else {
    next();
  }
});
```

If the path of the route being navigated to starts with */account* and the user isn't logged in, the user will be redirected to */login*; otherwise, `next()` will be called without any arguments, and they'll be able to see the account page they requested. It's important to remember to call `next()`; otherwise, the guard will never be resolved!

Checking the path in the guard can get tedious and confusing when you have a site with a lot of routes, so another feature you'll find useful here is *route meta fields*. You can add a `meta` property to the route, and then access it again from the guard. For example, let's set a `requiresAuth` property on the account route and check that in the guard instead:

```
const router = new VueRouter({
  routes: [
    {
      path: '/account',
      component: PageAccount,
      meta: {
        requiresAuth: true
      }
    }
  ]
});

router.beforeEach((to, from, next) => {
  if (to.meta.requiresAuth && !userAuthenticated()) {
    next('/login');
  } else {
    next();
  }
});
```

Now, whenever a user accesses *account*, the router will check the `requiresAuth` property of the router, and if the user isn't authenticated, will redirect them to the login page.

 When using nested routes, `to.meta` will equal the child component, not the parent. If you add the `meta` object to *account* and the user is accessing *account/email*, the `meta` object checked will be the one for the child, not the parent. To work around this, you can iterate through `to.matched`, which contains the parent routes as well:

```
router.beforeEach((to, from, next) => {
  const requiresAuth = to.matched.some((record) => {
    return record.meta.requiresAuth;
  }

  if (requiresAuth && !userAuthenticated()) {
    next('/login');
  } else {
    next();
  }
});
```

Now if you access `/account/email` and that route is a child route of `/account`, the `meta` objects for both of them will be checked, not just the `meta` object for `/account/email`.

In addition to `beforeEach`, which runs before navigation, an `afterEach` guard that runs afterward. Functions provided to this are passed only two arguments, `to` and `from`, and so cannot affect the navigation itself. It's a useful place to do stuff such as setting the page title, though:

```
const router = new VueRouter({
  routes: [
    {
      path: '/blog',
      component: PageBlog,
      meta: {
        title: 'Welcome to my blog!'
      }
    }
  ]
});

router.afterEach((to) => {
  document.title = to.meta.title;
});
```

That code will look at the `meta` attribute of the route every time page navigation occurs and set the page title to the `title` attribute of the `meta` object.

Per-Route Guards

In addition to defining `beforeEach` and `afterEach` guards on the router, you can define `beforeEnter` guards on individual routes:

```
const router = new VueRouter({
  routes: [
    {
      path: '/account',
      component: PageAccount,
      beforeEnter(to, from, next) {
        if (!userAuthenticated()) {
          next('/login');
        } else {
          next();
        }
      }
    }
  ]
});
```

These `beforeEnter` guards behave in exactly the same way as `beforeEach` guards, just applied only to individual routes instead of all of them.

In-Component Guards

Finally, you can also specify guards in components themselves. You can use three guards: `beforeRouteEnter` (the equivalent of `beforeEach`); `beforeRouteUpdate` (which you met earlier in this chapter); and `beforeRouteLeave` (which is called before navigating away from a route). All three of those guards accept the same three arguments as `beforeEach` and `beforeEnter`.

Let's take our previous authentication examples and apply the same logic in a component:

```
const PageAccount = {
  template: '<div>...account page...</div>',
  beforeRouteEnter(to, from, next) {
    if (!userAuthenticated()) {
      next('/login');
    } else {
      next();
    }
  }
};
```

Note that `this` is undefined in `beforeRouterEnter`, because the component hasn't been created yet. Instead, you can pass a callback to `next`, which will be passed the component as the first argument:

```
const PageAccount = {
  template: '<div>...account page...</div>',
  beforeRouteEnter(to, from, next) {
    next((vm) => {
      console.log(vm.$route);
    });
  }
};
```

You can use this in beforeRouteUpdate and beforeRouteLeave as you can in most
other places in the component, and so passing a callback to next isn't supported for
them.

Route Order

vue-router internally picks which route to display by going through the array of
routes and picking the first one that matches the current URL. Knowing this is
important—it means that the order of the routes is important. Take the following
routers:

```
const routerA = new VueRouter({
  routes: [
    {
      path: '/user/:userId',
      component: PageUser
    },
    {
      path: '/user/me',
      component: PageMe
    }
  ]
});

const routerB = new VueRouter({
  routes: [
    {
      path: '/user/me',
      component: PageMe
    },
    {
      path: '/user/:userId',
      component: PageUser
    }
  ]
});
```

They look similar: both of them define two routes, one for a user to access their own
page at */user/me* and another to access other users pages at */user/:userId*.

Using routerA, it is impossible to access PageMe. This is because vue-router has gone
through the router testing whether each path matches: if you access */user/me*, that

matches *user/:userId*, so userId is set to me and the PageUser component is displayed. With routerB, */user/me* matches first, so that component is used, and then anything else results in the PageUser route being displayed.

404 Pages

We can use the fact that vue-router searches through the routes in order with the wildcard operator (*) to display an error page when no other route has matched. To do that is as simple as follows:

```
const router = new VueRoute({
  routes: [
    // ...your other routes...
    {
      path: '*',
      component: PageNotFound
    }
  ]
});
```

The PageNotFound component will display when no other route has matched.

When using nested routes, if none of the child paths match, the router carries on looking down the array of routes outside the parent, so the same PageNotFound component will be used for them. If you want the error page to display in the parent component, you'll need to add the wildcard route to the array of child routes too:

```
const router = new VueRoute({
  routes: [
    {
      path: '/settings',
      component: PageSettings,
      children: [
        {
          path: 'profile',
          component: PageSettingsProfile
        },
        {
          path: '*',
          component: PageNotFound
        }
      ]
    }
    {
      path: '*',
      component: PageNotFound
    }
  ]
});
```

Now the same PageNotFound component will display, but with the sidebar from the PageSettings component too.

Route Names

The final feature of vue-router I'll cover in this chapter is the ability to give your routes names, and then use them to refer to your routes instead of their paths. Just add a `name` attribute to the route in the router:

```
const router = new VueRouter({
  routes: [
    {
      path: '/',
      name: 'home',
      component: PageHome
    },
    {
      path: '/user/:userId',
      name: 'user',
      component: PageUser
    }
  ]
});
```

Now instead of linking to the path, you can link using the name instead:

```
<router-link :to="{ name: 'home' }">Return to home</router-link>
```

The following two lines of code are equivalent:

```
<router-link to="/user/1234">User #1234</router-link>
<router-link :to="{ path: '/user/1234' }">
User #1234
</router-link>
```

The first is just short for the second.

You can use the same syntax with `router.push()`:

```
router.push({ name: 'home' });
```

Naming your routes and referring to them by using only their names instead of their paths means that the route and the path are no longer so tightly coupled: to change the path of a route, you have to change only the path in the router instead of having to go through all your existing links and updating them.

To link to a route with params such as the preceding `user` route, you can specify them in the `params` property of the object:

```
<router-link :to="{ name: 'user', params: { userId: 1234 }}">
User #1234
</router-link>
```

Summary

In this chapter, you looked at using vue-router to create a single-page application—an application with multiple pages in which the routing is handled client-side. You looked at various ways to configure a router, using dynamic routes to create dynamic paths; nested routes to create child routes; and redirects, aliases, and wildcard paths for 404 pages. You also looked at `<router-link>` to create links, named routes to almost entirely separate the path from the route, and navigation guards to run additional logic when a navigation event occurs.

CHAPTER 6

State Management with Vuex

Until this point in the book, all data has been stored in our components. We hit an API, and we store the returned data on the data object. We bind a form to an object, and we store that object on the data object. All communication between components has been done using events (to go from child to parent) and props (to go from parent to child). This is good for simple cases, but in more complicated applications, it won't suffice.

Let's take a social network app—specifically, messages. You want an icon in the top navigation to display the number of messages you have, and then you want a messages pop-up at the bottom of the page that will also tell you the number of messages you have. Both components are nowhere near each other on the page, so linking them using events and props would be a nightmare: components that are completely unrelated to notifications will have to be aware of the events to pass them through. The alternative is, instead of linking them together to share data, you could make separate API requests from each component. That would be even worse! Each component would update at different times, meaning they could be displaying different things, and the page would be making more API requests than it needed to.

vuex is a library that helps developers manage their application's state in Vue applications. It provides one centralized store that you can use throughout your app to store and work with global state, and gives you the ability to validate data going in to ensure that the data coming out again is predictable and correct.

Installation

You can use vuex via a CDN. Just add the following:

```
<script src="https://unpkg.com/vuex"></script>
```

Alternatively, if you're using npm, you can install vuex by using `npm install --save vuex`. If you're using a bundler such as webpack, then just as with vue-router, you have to call `Vue.use()`:

```
import Vue from 'vue';
import Vuex from 'vuex';

Vue.use(Vuex);
```

Then you need to set up your store. Let's create the following file and save it as *store/index.js*:

```
import Vuex from 'vuex';

export default new Vuex.Store({
  state: {}
});
```

For now, that's just an empty store: we'll add to it throughout the chapter.

Then, import it in your main app file and add it as a property when creating the Vue instance:

```
import Vue from 'vue';
import store from './store';

new Vue({
  el: '#app',
  store,
  components: {
    App
  }
});
```

You've now added the store to your app and you can access it using `this.$store`. Let's look at the concepts of vuex and then we'll look at what you can do with `this.$store`.

Concept

As mentioned in the introduction to this chapter, vuex can be required when complex applications require more than one component to share state.

Let's take a simple component written without vuex that displays the number of messages a user has on the page:

```
const NotificationCount = {
  template: `<p>Messages: {{ messageCount }}</p>`,
  data: () => ({
    messageCount: 'loading'
  }),
```

```
mounted() {
  const ws = new WebSocket('/api/messages');

  ws.addEventListener('message', (e) => {
    const data = JSON.parse(e.data);
    this.messageCount = data.messages.length;
  });
  }
};
```

It's pretty simple. It opens a websocket to */api/messages*, and then when the server
sends data to the client—in this case, when the socket is opened (initial message
count) and when the count is updated (on new messages)—the messages sent over
the socket are counted and displayed on the page.

 In practice, this code would be much more complicated: there's no
authentication on the websocket in this example, and it is always
assumed that the response over the websocket is valid JSON with a
messages property that is an array, when realistically it probably
wouldn't be. For this example, this simplistic code will do the job.

We run into problems when we want to use more than one of the Notification
Count components on the same page. As each component opens a websocket, it
opens unnecessary duplicate connections, and because of network latency, the components might update at slightly different times. To fix this, we can move the websocket logic into vuex.

Let's dive right in with an example. Our component will become this:

```
const NotificationCount = {
  template: `<p>Messages: {{ messageCount }}</p>`,
  computed: {
    messageCount() {
      return this.$store.state.messages.length;
    }
  }
  mounted() {
    this.$store.dispatch('getMessages');
  }
};
```

And the following will become our vuex store:

```
let ws;

export default new Vuex.Store({
  state: {
    messages: [],
  },
  mutations: {
```

```
      setMessages(state, messages) {
        state.messages = messages;
      }
    },
    actions: {
      getMessages({ commit }) {
        if (ws) {
          return;
        }

        ws = new WebSocket('/api/messages');

        ws.addEventListener('message', (e) => {
          const data = JSON.parse(e.data);
          commit('setMessages', data.messages);
        });
      }
    }
});
```

Now, every notification count component that is mounted will trigger `getMessages`, but the action checks whether the websocket exists and opens a connection only if there isn't one already open. Then it listens to the socket, committing changes to the state, which will then be updated in the notification count component as the store is reactive—just like most other things in Vue. When the socket sends down something new, the global store will be updated, and every component on the page will be updated at the same time.

Throughout the rest of the chapter, I'll introduce the individual concepts you saw in that example—state, mutations, and actions—and explain a way we can structure our vuex modules in large applications to avoid having one large, messy file.

State and State Helpers

First, let's look at state. *State* indicates how data is stored in our vuex store. It's like one big object that we can access from anywhere in our application—it's the *single source of truth*.

Let's take a simple store that contains only a number:

```
import Vuex from 'vuex';

export default new Vuex.Store({
  state: {
    messageCount: 10
  }
});
```

Now, in our application, we can access the `messageCount` property of the state object by accessing `this.$store.state.messageCount`. This is a bit verbose, so generally it's better to put it in a computed property, like so:

```
const NotificationCount = {
  template: `<p>Messages: {{ messageCount }}</p>`,
  computed: {
    messageCount() {
      return this.$store.state.messageCount;
    }
  }
};
```

Now, the component will display "Messages: 10".

State Helpers

Accessing the store in a computed property is fine when you're referring to only a couple of properties of the store, but it can get repetitive if you're referring to lots of them. For this reason, vuex provides a `mapState` helper that returns an object of functions that can be used as computed properties.

Generally, all you need to provide is an array of strings:

```
import { mapState } from 'vuex';

const NotificationCount = {
  template: `<p>Messages: {{ messageCount }}</p>`,
  computed: mapState(['messageCount'])
};
```

That does the same as the code example before, but is much shorter. If we have more properties we want to get from the vuex store, we can simply add their names to the `mapState` call.

The preceding `mapState` call is short for the following:

```
computed: mapState({
  messageCount: (state) => state.messageCount
})
```

The `mapState` function takes an object for which every key corresponds to a computed property. If it is given a function, the function is called with `state` as the first argument, and you can retrieve the value you want from it. You can also give it a string if you're just getting a property from the state:

```
computed: mapState({
  messageCount: 'messageCount'
})
```

You've just looked at three ways of getting the exact same value from the store and making it available as the exact same computed property; you might be wondering about the difference between them.

If every one of your mappings is a simple mapping from the same computed property name to the property name in vuex—for example, `messageCount` corresponds to `state.messageCount`—you can use the array syntax demonstrated in the first example.

If, however, any of the properties are going to be mapped to different names or need processing, you need to use the full object syntax. Then I'd recommend using the string syntax wherever possible—it's a lot easier to read—and the function syntax whenever you need to do processing. For example, if we have a `messages` property of the state that stores an array of messages and we want the length as `messageCount`, we can do the following:

```
computed: mapState({
  messageCount: (state) => state.messages.length,
  somethingElse: 'somethingElse'
})
```

It is, of course, up to you which style you use.

If using the full function syntax, not ES6 fat-arrow functions, you can also access the component as `this` to combine both component state and vuex state:

```
computed: mapState({
  messageCount(state) {
    return state.messages.length + this.pendingMessages.length;
  }
})
```

 In the previous example, we mixed vuex state and local state. A common mistake people make when using vuex is moving *all* their application state into vuex, which isn't something you want to do. It's fine to still use local state and best to combine the two: application state shared between multiple components into vuex, and simple state that's used in only one component in local state.

Finally, let's look at a way to combine `mapState` with your existing computed properties. As it returns an object, if you have any existing computed properties, you need a way to merge the two objects together. Luckily, there's a stage 3 ECMAScript proposal (meaning that it's a candidate for inclusion into JavaScript) which can help us here: the object spread operator. It's like the array spread operator in ECMAScript 2015, but for objects:

```
computed: {
  doubleFoo() {
```

```
    return this.foo * 2;
  },
  ...mapState({
      messageCount: (state) => state.messages.length,
      somethingElse: 'somethingElse'
    })
}
```

The resulting object for this example is as follows:

```
computed: {
  doubleFoo() {
    return this.foo * 2;
  },
  messageCount() {
    return this.$store.state.messages.length,
  },
  somethingElse() {
    return this.$store.state.somethingElse;
  }
}
```

Note that if you use the object spread operator, you'll want to use a transpilation tool such as Babel to ensure maximum browser support.

Getters

Sometimes you might find that you're using the same data in multiple components and doing the same processing in all of them, resulting in duplicate code. For example, maybe we're finding ourselves calculating the name of the people we haven't read messages from repeatedly:

```
computed: mapState({
  unreadFrom: (state) => state
    .filter((message) => !message.read)
    .map((message) => message.user.name)
})
```

That might be fine if we're using the computed property only once, but if we're using it in multiple components, that's a lot of repetition. If the API schema changes (maybe `message.user.name` is changed to `message.sender.full_name`), then we'll have to update our code in a lot of places.

Luckily, vuex provides us with getters, which allow us to move the code we're commonly reusing into our vuex store to avoid duplicating it elsewhere.

Let's look at how we might move the code from the preceding example into our vuex store:

```
import Vuex from 'vuex';
```

```
export default new Vuex.Store({
  state: {
    messages: [...]
  },
  getters: {
    unreadFrom: (state) => state.messages
      .filter((message) => !message.read)
      .map((message) => message.user.name)
  }
});
```

Now the unreadFrom getter can be accessed at store.getters.unreadFrom:

```
computed: {
  unreadFrom() {
    return this.$store.getters.unreadFrom;
  }
}
```

Neat. Getters can also access other getters by using their second argument. For example, let's split the previous getter into two smaller getters:

```
import Vuex from 'vuex';

export default new Vuex.Store({
  state: {
    messages: [...]
  },
  getters: {
    unread: (state) => state.filter((message) => !message.read),
    unreadFrom: (state, getters) => getters.unread
      .map((message) => message.user.name)
  }
});
```

Getter Helpers

Just as with state, there are helpers for getter methods instead of typing this. $store.getters every time. It works similarly to mapState, but doesn't support the function syntax.

There's an array syntax

```
computed: mapGetters(['unread', 'unreadFrom'])
```

that's the equivalent of the following:

```
computed: {
  unread() {
    return this.$store.getters.unread;
  },
  unreadFrom() {
    return this.$store.getters.unreadFrom;
```

```
    },
  }
```

And there's an object syntax

```
computed: mapGetters({
  unreadMessages: 'unread',
  unreadMessagesFrom: 'unreadFrom'
})
```

that is the equivalent of the following:

```
computed: {
  unreadMessages() {
    return this.$store.getters.unread;
  },
  unreadMessagesFrom() {
    return this.$store.getters.unreadFrom;
  },
}
```

Mutations

So far you've looked only at how to get data out of the store, not at how to modify the data. You can't just modify the values in the state object directly; you have to use a mutation to do it.

A *mutation* is a function that synchronously modifies the state and is invoked by calling `store.commit()` with the name of the mutation.

Now, let's create a mutation that allows us to add a message to the end of the array of messages:

```
import Vuex from 'vuex';

export default new Vuex.Store({
  state: {
    messages: []
  },
  mutations: {
    addMessage(state, newMessage) {
      state.messages.push(newMessage);
    }
  }
});
```

Then to add a message, we can call `store.commit()` in our component:

```
const SendMessage = {
  template: '<form @submit="handleSubmit">...</form>',
  data: () => ({
    formData: { ... }
  }),
```

```
methods: {
  handleSubmit() {
    this.$store.commit('addMessage', this.formData);
  }
}
};
```

The first argument of the commit method is the name of the mutation, and the second is an optional argument known as the *payload*.

The method also supports an object syntax:

```
this.$store.commit({
  type: 'addMessage',
  newMessage: this.formData
});
```

The entire object will be the payload, so the mutation would have to change to push payload.newMessage instead of the entire payload.

Mutation Helpers

Just as with state and getters, there's a mapMutations method for mutations too. It has the exact same syntax as the mapGetters helper.

There's an array syntax

```
methods: mapMutations(['addMessage'])
```

that's the equivalent of the following:

```
methods: {
  addMessage(payload) {
    return this.$store.commit('addMessage', payload);
  },
}
```

As you can see, it also supports payloads (again, optionally).

Plus, there's an object syntax if you want the names of the methods to be different from the names of the mutations:

```
methods: mapMutations({
  addNewMessage: 'addMessage'
})
```

That is the equivalent of the following:

```
methods: {
  addNewMessage(payload) {
    return this.$store.commit('addMessage', payload);
  },
}
```

Mutations Must Be Synchronous

As I mentioned before, mutations are only for performing *synchronous* changes to the state object. If you want to make an asynchronous change, you need to use an *action*.

Actions

Finally, we have actions. You can make only synchronous changes with mutations, so actions are used for making asynchronous changes.

Let's make an action that builds on the state and mutations you've seen previously. The action will call the server by using the `fetch` API, check whether there are new messages, and push any new messages to the end of the `messages` array:

```
import Vuex from 'vuex';

export default new Vuex.Store({
  state: {
    messages: []
  },
  mutations: {
    addMessage(state, newMessage) {
      state.messages.push(newMessage);
    },
    addMessages(state, newMessages) {
      state.messages.push(...newMessages);
    }
  },
  actions: {
    getMessages(context) {
      fetch('/api/new-messages')
        .then((res) => res.json())
        .then((data) => {
          if (data.messages.length) {
            context.commit('addMessages', data.messages);
          }
        });
    }
  }
});
```

There are two new things in this code example: first an `addMessages` mutation, which is similar to the `addMessage` mutation but can add more than one message at once, and the `getMessages` action, which checks the server for new messages, and if there are any, calls the `addMessages` mutation with those new messages.

Then, to call `getMessages` in our component, we use the `store.dispatch()` method. Let's add a little link to the `NotificationCount` component to update the message count:

```
import { mapState } from 'vuex';

const NotificationCount = {
  template: `<p>
    Messages: {{ messages.length }}
    <a @click.prevent="handleUpdate">(update)</a>
  </p>`,
  computed: mapState(['messages']),
  methods: {
    handleUpdate() {
      this.$store.dispatch('getMessages');
    }
  }
};
```

Now, clicking the link results in the following process:

1. When the link is clicked, the `handleUpdate` method is fired.

2. The `getMessages` action is dispatched.

3. A request is sent to */api/new-messages*.

4. When that request returns, if it has new messages, the `addMessages` mutation will be called with the new messages as a payload.

5. The `addMessages` mutation pushes the new messages to the `messages` property of the state.

6. Because the state is reactive, the `messages` computed property updates, and the text display on the page changes.

`dispatch` takes the same syntax as `commit`: it can either have the name of the action as the first argument and the payload as the second argument, or it can take an object with a `type` property, which will also be used as the payload.

Action Helpers

As with everything else covered so far in this chapter, actions have a `mapActions` helper that you can use to map methods to actions:

```
methods: {
  // Maps this.getMessage() to this.$store.dispatch('getMessage')
  ...mapActions(['getMessage'])

  // Maps this.update() to this.$store.dispatch('getMessages')
  ...mapActions({
    update: 'getMessages'
  })
}
```

Destructuring

It's fairly standard in actions to use destructuring in the arguments instead of referring to context, like so:

```
actions: {
  getMessages({ commit }) {
    // Do some stuff, then…
    commit('addMessages', data.messages);
  }
}
```

context equals the vuex store—or, as you're about to explore in the next section—the current vuex module. You can access the state through it (it's just the state property), but you can't mutate it—you need to use mutations for that.

Promises and Actions

Actions are asynchronous, so how do we know when they're finished? We could watch the computed property for changes, but that isn't ideal.

Instead, we can return a promise inside the action. Then, the call to dispatch will also return a promise, which we can use to run code when the action has finished running.

Let's change our previous getMessages action so that it returns a promise:

```
actions: {
  getMessages({ commit }) {
    return fetch('/api/new-messages')
      .then((res) => res.json())
      .then((data) => {
        if (data.messages.length) {
          commit('addMessages', data.messages);
        }
      });
  }
}
```

It's a small change—just a return keyword before the fetch call. Now, let's change our NotificationCount component to display a loading sign when the message count is being updated. To do that, we'll need to add an updating property to the local state of the component that will equal true or false:

```
import { mapState } from 'vuex';

const NotificationCount = {
  template: `<p>
              Messages: {{ messages.length }}
              <span v-if="loading">(updating…)</span>
```

```
                <a v-else @click.prevent="handleUpdate">(update)</a>
              </p>`,
    data: () => ({
      updating: false,
    }),
    computed: mapState(['messages']),
    methods: {
      handleUpdate() {
        this.updating = true;
        this.$store.dispatch('getMessages')
          .then(() => {
            this.updating = false;
          });
      }
    }
};
```

Now, when the component is updating, the component displays (updating…) instead of the link to update the message count.

Modules

Now that you know how to store and manipulate data in a vuex store, let's talk a bit about how to structure your store.

In smaller apps, the way you've seen so far—keeping all of your state, getters, mutations, and actions in one file—works great. In larger applications, however, that can get a bit messy, so vuex allows you to split your store into modules.

Each *module* is just an object, and has its own state, getters, mutations, and actions, and is then added to the store by using the modules property. Let's take our previous store and split out the messages logic (so, all of it) into a module:

```
import Vuex from 'vuex';

const messages = {
  state: {
    messages: []
  },
  mutations: {
    addMessage(state, newMessage) {
      state.messages.push(newMessage);
    },
    addMessages(state, newMessages) {
      state.messages.push(...newMessages);
    }
  },
  actions: {
    return getMessages({ commit }) {
      fetch('/api/new-messages')
        .then((res) => res.json())
```

```
          .then((data) => {
            if (data.messages.length) {
              commit('addMessages', data.messages);
            }
          });
      }
    }
  };

  export default new Vuex.Store({
    modules: {
      messages,
    }
  });
```

After this modification, a couple of subtle changes occur in the way it works now.

The first one is that `state` in the mutation and getters now refers to the module state instead of the root state (the state of the main store), and `context` in the actions refers to the module instead of the store. Everything you do in that module affects only that module, and not any other modules. In getters, you can access the root scope by using the third `rootScope` property, and in actions you can access the root scope by using the `rootScope` property of the `scope` object.

The second change is that you now need to specify the module when retrieving data from the store. You now need to access `state.messages.messages` (instead of `state.messages`), where the first `messages` is the name of the namespace, and the second is the name of the property in the state.

We don't need to worry about the first change in this case—everything still works as expected—but the second change requires us to make a change to the `mapState` call in the `NotificationCount` component. We can just add the name of the module as the first argument:

```
computed: mapState('messages', ['messages'])
```

This does mean that if you're getting state from more than one module, you'll have to call `mapState` multiple times, but with the object spread operator, that's not a big issue.

File Structure

Generally, I like to split each module into its own file. This makes the code a bit neater and more organized, and also means that the ES6 export syntax can be used to make the module itself really clean. Let's move the messages code into its own file, saved in *store/modules/messages.js*:

```
export const state = {
  messages: []
```

```
  };

  export const mutations = {
    addMessage(state, newMessage) {
      state.messages.push(newMessage);
    },
    addMessages(state, newMessages) {
      state.messages.push(...newMessages);
    }
  };

  export const actions = {
    return getMessages({ commit }) {
      fetch('/api/new-messages')
        .then((res) => res.json())
        .then((data) => {
          if (data.messages.length) {
            commit('addMessages', data.messages);
          }
        });
    }
  };
```

You can then import it in *store/index.js* as follows:

```
import Vuex from 'vuex';
import * as messages from './modules/messages';

export default new Vuex.Store({
  modules: {
    messages,
  }
});
```

You can, of course, keep the module as one object and a default export (that's how it is in the official documentation); I just find it a bit nicer this way.

Namespaced Modules

By default, only the state of a vuex module is namespaced. Getters, mutations, and actions are still called in exactly the same way, and if an action is dispatched that exists in multiple modules, it's run on all the modules it's found on. This can be useful sometimes, but it could potentially be an accident. It's possible to namespace the entire module to prevent this from happening.

To tell vuex to namespace the module, add a namespaced: true property to the object—or in the case of our previous example in its own file, add the following:

```
export const namespaced = true;
```

Now to access getters, specify the namespace name in the string before their name:

```
computed: {
  unreadFrom() {
    return this.$store.getters['messages/unreadFrom'];
  }
}
```

To trigger mutations and dispatch actions, do the same again—specify the namespace name in the string before their name:

```
store.commit('messages/addMessage', newMessage);

store.dispatch('messages/getMessages');
```

Just as with `mapState`, the other three helpers—`mapGetters`, `mapMutations`, and `mapActions`—accept the name of the module as the first argument.

Let's take a look at what namespacing the module does to our `NotificationCount` component:

```
import { mapState } from 'vuex';

const NotificationCount = {
  template: `<p>
              Messages: {{ messages.length }}
              <span v-if="loading">(updating…)</span>
              <a v-else @click.prevent="handleUpdate">(update)</a>
            </p>`,
  data: () => ({
    updating: false,
  }),
  computed: mapState('messages', ['messages']),
  methods: {
    handleUpdate() {
      this.updating = true;
      this.$store.dispatch('messages/getMessages')
        .then(() => {
          this.updating = false;
        });
    }
  }
};
```

Nothing huge has changed, but it's now clear that the module is namespaced.

Summary

In this chapter, you looked at using vuex to manage complicated application state and the various concepts of vuex:

- The vuex store is where everything—state, getters, mutations, and actions—are stored and accessed through.

- State is the object where all your data is stored.

- Getters allow you to store common logic used to retrieve data from the store.

- Mutations are used to synchronously change data in the store.

- Actions are used to asynchronously change data in the store.

State, getters, mutations, and actions also have helpers to help you add them to your components, named `mapState`, `mapGetters`, `mapMutations`, and `mapActions`, respectively.

Finally, you also looked at using modules to divide your vuex store into logical chunks.

CHAPTER 7

Testing Vue Components

By separating our code into components, we've made it easy to write unit tests for our app. Our code has been divided into small chunks that serve one purpose each, with a relatively small number of options—perfect for testing. Testing your code ensures that when you make changes in the future, you won't break things that you weren't expecting to have changed. If you're working on any reasonably sized app, you should probably be writing tests.

In this chapter, we'll first look at testing your components using just Vue, and then we'll look at using vue-test-utils to make the syntax a bit nicer.

We won't be looking at a test framework such as Jasmine, Mocha, or Jest in this book. The most the tests written in this chapter will do is throw an error that can then be inspected in the browser console. For a more in-depth look at testing in JavaScript, check out *JavaScript Testing with Jasmine* (*http://oreil.ly/ZEgmw9*) by Evan Hahn (O'Reilly), or any number of articles online.

Testing a Simple Component

Let's start by looking at a simple component that we can test—a simpler version of the NotificationCount component you saw in the previous chapter:

```
const NotificationCount = {
  template: `<p>
    Messages: <span class="count">{{ messageCount }}</span>
    <a @click.prevent="handleUpdate">(update)</a>
  </p>`,
  props: {
    initialCount: {
      type: Number,
      default: 0
    }
```

```
    },
    data() {
      return { messageCount: this.initialCount };
    },
    methods: {
      handleUpdate() {
        this.$http.get('/api/new-messages')
          .then((data) => {
            this.messageCount += data.messages.length;
          });
      }
    }
  };
```

The component initially displays the notification count given in the `initialCount` prop, and then calls an API to update the number whenever the update link is pressed.

But what could we test? I can see three things that we could write tests for:

- We could test that the provided initial count displays correctly.
- There could be a test to ensure that when the update link is clicked, the count updates correctly.
- Finally, there could be a test to make sure that the component gracefully handles failure from the API (it currently doesn't).

For now, let's not worry about testing the update functionality and just look at the initial count.

To test the `NotificationCount` component, we can create a new Vue instance in which `NotificationCount` is the only child:

```
const vm = new Vue({
  template: '<NotificationCount :initial-count="5" />',
  components: { NotificationCount }
}).$mount();
```

Because we didn't provide `new Vue()` with an `el` property, we need to call `.$mount()` manually so that Vue starts the mounting process. Otherwise, we can't test our component properly.

> vm is short for ViewModel, and is commonly used throughout this book, the vue-test-utils documentation, and the Vue.js documentation itself.

If you log vm to the console, you can see that it is an object with a ton of properties. The one we care about right now is the $el property, which is the element generated by Vue.

Logging vm.$el.outerHTML to the console results in the following:

```
<p>
      Messages: <span class="count">5</span>
      <a>(update)</a></p>
```

We can see that the initial count has displayed properly, but let's write some code that throws an error if it hasn't so that we don't have to check the HTML manually every time. vm.$el is a standard DOM node, so we can use .querySelector() on it to find the .count span:

```
const count = vm.$el.querySelector('.count').innerHTML;

if (count !== '5') {
   thrown new Error('Expected count to equal "5"');
}
```

If we add an assertion library such as Chai, we can simplify the second part into something you're probably more familiar with if you have written tests before:

```
const count = vm.$el.querySelector('.count').innerHTML;
expect(count).toBe('5');
```

If the displayed count is anything other than 5 now, an error will be thrown, and the test will fail.

Introducing vue-test-utils

The syntax in the preceding example is a bit more verbose than it needs to be, and that is just a simple example. With more complicated examples involving events and mocked components, you almost end up writing more code to test a component than is in the component itself!

vue-test-utils is an official Vue library to assist you writing tests. It provides functionality to perform the repetitive parts of writing Vue components such as querying the DOM, setting props and data, mocking components and other properties, and working with events.

It doesn't help you with testing running (for that, use a library such as Jest or Mocha) or assertions (for that, try Chai or Should.js), so you'll need to install them separately. I don't cover test runners in this chapter. I'll just write some code that will throw an error if the test fails and assume that there will be something to catch the error.

To install vue-test-utils, you can use unpckg or another CDN as with the other libraries, but generally you're going to want to install it from npm:

```
$ npm install --save-dev vue-test-utils
```

Now, in your test file, you can import vue-test-utils and rewrite the test as follows:

```
import { mount } from 'vue-test-utils'

const wrapper = mount(NotificationCount, {
  propsData: {
    initialCount: 5
  }
});

const count = wrapper.find('.count').text();
expect(count).toBe('5');
```

Although this code isn't any shorter—in fact, it's pretty much the same length—it's much easier to read. Larger examples are often significantly shorter when written using vue-test-utils too.

Querying the DOM

In the previous example, you saw the following expression:

```
wrapper.find('.count').text()
```

But what is that doing?

First, let's go back to the `mount()` function. This function takes the component and some options—in this case, just props data—and returns a *wrapper*, which is an object provided by vue-test-utils that wraps a mounted component and allows us to run operations on and query the component without having to use the browser's native DOM methods too much.

One of the methods provided by the wrapper is the `.find()` method, which when provided with a selector will query the element that corresponds to the wrapped element and finds the first element in the DOM that matches that selector. Basically, it's the equivalent of `.querySelector()` on a DOM element. After `.find()` has located the element, it returns that element wrapped in another wrapper—not the element itself.

 Note that `.find()` returns only the first element matching the selector. If you want more than one, use `.findAll()`. This returns a `WrapperArray` object, not a `Wrapper`, but it has similar methods, with the addition of an `.at()` method to return just the element at the given index in a wrapper.

Now that we have the `.count` span in a wrapper, we need another method to read the contents of the element to test what it is equal to. There are two methods we could use for this, .html() and .text(), but it's generally better to use .text() where possible so we'll use that here.

We now have the contents of the .count span stored in a variable and can test it by using whatever method we prefer.

You can use quite a few functions to query the DOM, and they will probably have changed or been added to by the time you read this book, so there's no point covering them all here; go check out the documentation!

mount() Options

You saw that we can provide an object as the second argument to mount() and tell Vue what props we want the component to have with it, but there's a lot more we can do with it. You can see a full list in the Vue.js and vue-test-utils documentation, but here are a few of the most useful:

propsData (as you saw before) is used to pass props to our component:

```
const wrapper = mount(NotificationCount, {
  propsData: {
    initialCount: 5
  }
});
```

slots is used to pass components or HTML strings to the component. Let's mount our blog post component from the "Named Slots" on page 53:

```
const wrapper = mount(BlogPost, {
  slots: {
    default: BlogContentComponent,
    header: '<h2>Blog post title</h2>'
  },
  propsData: {
    author: blogAuthor
  }
});
```

mocks is used to add properties to the instance. For example, in the first example in this chapter, we used this.$http.get() to send an HTTP request. Let's create a mock for that API:

```
const wrapper = mount(NotificationsCount, {
  mocks: {
    $http: {
      get() {
        return Promise.resolve({ messageCount: 2 });
      }
    }
  },
  propsData: {
```

```
      initialCount: 0
   }
});
```

Now instead of calling an actual API (which would be brittle and far too slow for unit tests), calling `this.$http.get('/api/new-messages')` will return a promise that resolves immediately.

`listeners` is an object containing functions to be used as event listeners. Often you don't need to use this option, as the `emitted` property of the wrapper object will suffice, but we'll explore that in "Working with Events" on page 127:

```
const wrapper = mount(Counter, {
  listeners: {
    count(clicks) {
      console.log(`Clicked ${clicks} times`);
    }
  }
});
```

`stubs` is similar to `mocks`, but instead of mocking variables, you can use it to stub components:

```
const wrapper = mount(TheSidebar, {
  stubs: {
    'sidebar-content': FakeSidebarContent
  }
});
```

As I said, those are just some of the options I've found most useful: more are covered in the official documentation.

Mocking and Stubbing Data

The previous section briefly covered the `mocks` option, which allows you to add properties to the instance to mock functionality that has been added to `Vue.fn` to make it accessible everywhere in your Vue instance. We also covered the `stubs` option, which allows you to put in a fake component or HTML instead of having to depend on another real component in your tests. Both options reduce the complexity of your tests by reducing the number of moving parts that your component is depending on; if you break one component, you ideally don't want all the tests for components depending on that component to start failing as well!

There are also four `.set*()` methods you can use to set the props, data, computed properties, and methods of a component. `.setComputed()` and `.setMethods()` are great methods for overriding computed properties and methods, possibly simplifying what you need to mock that the method would have called later.

Instead of overriding the this.$http.get() function on the NotificationsCount method, for example, we could have overridden the entire handleUpdate method to increase the message count by two:

```
const wrapper = mount(NotificationsCount, {
  propsData: {
    initialCount: 0
  }
});

wrapper.setMethods({
  handleUpdate() {
    this.messageCount += 2;
  }
});
```

Be careful when doing this—it can make your tests quite brittle—but when applied carefully, it can be a super useful feature.

setComputed() behaves similarly, but you give it a specific value, not a function:

```
const wrapper = mount(NumberTotal);

wrapper.setComputed({
  numberTotal: 16
});
```

Working with Events

Finally, vue-test-utils contains functionality that makes it easier for you to work with events. This is where I find vue-test-utils most useful: this isn't that trivial without the library.

First, let's take a look at how to trigger events on a component. Remember that our NotificationCount component had a link to update the message count: let's write a test that clicks that link and then checks that the event has been triggered.

To test whether the link has been clicked, let's mock this.$http with a method that returns a promise (as before), but also sets a variable to true to show that it has been called:

```
let clicked = false;

const wrapper = mount(NotificationsCount, {
  mocks: {
    $http: {
      get() {
        clicked = true;
        return Promise.resolve({ messageCount: 1 });
      }
    }
```

```
    },
    propsData: {
      initialCount: 2
    }
  });
```

Now, when the update is triggered, `clicked` should be changed to `true`.

Wrapper objects have a `.trigger()` method we can use to trigger a click event:

```
wrapper.find('a').trigger('click');
```

Now, we can test that `clicked` is `true`—if it isn't, the test should fail:

```
expect(clicked).toBe(true);
```

Finally, let's look at how we can see which custom events have been fired by components. Every wrapper object stores all the events that have been emitted on it, and you can access it by using the `.emitted()` method. This is super useful and means that you don't have to worry about adding event listeners: they're all already being captured!

In "Custom Events" on page 56, you met a component called `Counter` that emits a `count` event containing the number of times it has been clicked every time it is clicked. Let's write a test to check whether the number is accurate:

```
const wrapper = mount(Counter);

// Click three times
wrapper.find('button').trigger('click');
wrapper.find('button').trigger('click');
wrapper.find('button').trigger('click');

const emitted = wrapper.emitted();

expect(emitted.count).toBeTruthy();
expect(emitted.count.length).toBe(3);

expect(emitted.count[0]).toBe(1);
expect(emitted.count[1]).toBe(2);
expect(emitted.count[2]).toBe(3);
```

We can see not only what events have been emitted, but also the payload that was emitted with them and the order they were emitted in. This is useful when debugging components that emit events.

An `emittedByOrder()` method behaves similarly but contains an array instead, so that you can see the order in which all the events were fired, not just the events with the same name.

Summary

In this final chapter, you looked at how to take everything you've learned about Vue components so far in this book and write unit tests for them using another official Vue library called vue-test-utils. The library wraps your Vue components and provides useful methods that allow you to stub and mock components, libraries,. and properties, pass in mock data and props, access and manipulate properties of the generated elements, and trigger and capture events.

Bootstrapping Vue

Setting up Vue from scratch with a build tool, tests, and all the libraries required to write a large application can be an educational experience that everyone should attempt once. However, realistically, it can be a pain and is probably not something you want to do every time you set up Vue. You can set up a fully functional Vue install in numerous ways without having to set it up yourself, and this short appendix covers some of them.

vue-cli

vue-cli enables you to quickly bootstrap Vue applications from various provided templates. I used to set up pretty much every Vue project I work on.

To install vue-cli:

```
$ npm install --global vue-cli
```

Then, pick the template that you want to install and run npm init [*template name*]. For example, to use the webpack template, run the following:

```
$ vue init webpack
```

You'll then be presented with a setup wizard, which asks a series of questions such as where you want to set up your project, what libraries you want to be installed, and some npm setup information.

Depending on what template you choose, it'll look something like this:

```
❯ vue init webpack

? Generate project in current directory? Yes
? Project name vue-test
? Project description A Vue.js project
? Author Callum Macrae <callum@macr.ae>
? Vue build standalone
? Install vue-router? No
? Use ESLint to lint your code? No
? Setup unit tests with Karma + Mocha? No
? Setup e2e tests with Nightwatch? No

  vue-cli · Generated "vue-test".

  To get started:

    npm install
    npm run dev

  Documentation can be found at https://vuejs-templates.github.io/webpack
```

Once you've installed the dependencies of your new project, you can run the startup command it gives you (for the webpack template, it's npm run dev), and you'll be able to dive in with a fully setup application that requires very little configuration to get to where you want it.

Several officially provided templates are available for Vue. They're all stored on the vuejs-templates organization on GitHub. Presented in order based on the number of GitHub stars, the six available templates at the time of writing are described in the following sections.

webpack

The webpack template is the most starred on GitHub, and from what I've seen also the most commonly used. It provides a fully featured webpack setup with vue-loader for single-file components (.vue files), hot module reloading, and linting, and can set you up with vue-router, unit tests, and functional tests if you want them.

pwa

This template is based on the webpack template and does everything it does, but also sets up your application to be used as a progressive web application—a web app that is available offline and is designed to be saved to the home screen of a user's mobile device.

webpack-simple

This template is like the webpack template, but simpler. It provides only a simple webpack setup with vue-loader and other essential loaders, but doesn't set up anything like hot module reloading, linting, or any of the optional modules the webpack template installs.

I do not recommend using this template. If you want a simpler setup, use the webpack template and select "No" for all the options you don't want. This template isn't designed for production usage, so if you decide that you want to use the project as more than a prototype, you'll have to redo your webpack setup.

simple

The simple template contains just an HTML file and a CSS file. It's super simple, and great for when a build system is overkill.

browserify

The browserify template provides a fully featured Browserify setup. It provides you with vueify to use single-file components with Browserify, hot module reloading, and linting, and optionally vue-router, unit tests, and functional tests.

browserify-simple

Much like webpack-simple, this is a minimal version of the browserify template.

Your Own Template

It's also possible to make your own template. If none of the templates work for you or you find yourself making the same changes every time you use one of the provided templates (for example, I always find myself adding semicolons to the build files of the webpack template), this might be best for you. You can either fork one of the existing templates or start completely from scratch; the documentation for vue-cli explains how you can do this.

Nuxt.js

As an alternative to vue-cli, you can use Nuxt.js to set up your Vue applications. It allows you to create a client-side application while abstracting away all the configuration. It sets up Vue, vue-router, vuex, vue-meta (used for easily setting stuff such as page titles), with webpack and Babel. It also sets up server-side rendering, automatic code splitting, CSS preprocessing, static file serving, and a ton of other useful features.

Vue from React

If you've used React before, you're probably already familiar with a lot of the concepts in Vue. I've compiled a list of some of the similarities and differences between the two frameworks in this appendix. This section is fairly heavily example based: it's a lot easier to understand the differences and similarities from examples than from me writing about it!

Getting Started

Both Vue and React have similar tools that you can use to set up a simple app. React has create-react-app, which sets up a webpack configuration to build a React app and then hides the configuration from you. Vue has vue-cli, which has various templates that you can use to install Vue with webpack, Browserify, or without any build tool at all. The vue-cli templates are also configurable and will set up vue-router, unit testing, and functional testing (but not vuex) if you want it to—something that create-react-app will not provide.

You can also build your own templates to use with vue-cli. Check out Appendix A for more information on vue-cli and the templates available to you.

There's also a difference in setup when you want just a simple setup. React doesn't work great without a build tool, because you can't write JSX without a parser; it's not supported in the browser. Nearly every React project uses webpack, and Browserify support is limited. Vue doesn't require JSX (although you can use it if you want it), so it's possible to use it in the browser without a build tool. Most projects don't do this, as having a module bundler and an ES2015 transpiler is generally required in all projects, but it's nice to have the option. It's also great for beginners, as you can start writing Vue without having to worry about a complicated build setup.

Similarities

Many similarities exist between React and Vue. Vue was designed to take the best bits of Angular and React and combine them, so if there's a thing you really like about React, chances are you'll be able to find it in Vue too. This section explains and demonstrates some of the similarities.

Components

Both React and Vue are heavily component-driven. Using components is a great way of working: it allows you to split your application into sensible, reusable chunks that are each responsible for a distinct part of your application. This makes them easy to test too. Every component in both React and Vue has its own state: in React, it's called *state* and stored using the setState() method, and in Vue, it's called *data*, and is stored by mutating the data object. You can also pass data into components, which is done basically the same way in both libraries and called *props*. The syntax is slightly different, but that is covered in "Differences" on page 141.

Let's demonstrate with a simple component that accepts a user ID as a prop, and then makes an API request and displays the resulting user data on the page.

Here's the component in React:

```
class UserView extends React.Component {
  constructor(props) {
    super(props);

    this.state = {
      user: undefined
    };

    fetch(`/api/user/${this.props.userId}`)
      .then((res) => res.json())
      .then((user) => {
        this.setState({ user });
      });
  },
  render() {
    const user = this.state.user;

    return (
      <div>
        { user ? (
          <p>User name: {user.name}</p>
        ) : (
          <p>Loading...</p>
        ) }
      </div>
    );
```

```
    }
};

UserView.propTypes = {
  userId: PropTypes.number
};
```

And here it is in Vue:

```
const UserView = {
  template: `
    <div>
      <p v-if="user">User name: {{ user.name }}</p>
      <p v-else>Loading...</p>
    </div>`,
  props: {
    userId: {
      type: Number,
      required: true
    }
  },
  data: () => ({
    user: undefined
  },
  mounted() {
    fetch(`/api/user/${this.userId}`)
      .then((res) => res.json())
      .then((user) => {
        this.user = user;
      });
  }
};
```

Both components are called in similar ways.

In React:

```
<UserGuide userId={10} />
```

And in Vue:

```
<UserGuide :userId="10" />
```

Both React and Vue have one-way data flow. You can pass data into components using props, but you cannot modify props directly.

Reactivity

Both React and Vue have similar reactivity mechanisms. Reactivity was one of the best things about React, so it's great that Vue has it too!

When you update the state in React or the data in Vue, or when a prop or one of any of the things the library is watching changes, everything that depends on that value is updated. For example, if you have a state that is passed into a component as a prop and displayed in the DOM, when the state changes, the prop will be updated, and the inner component will know that the prop has changed and update the value in the DOM.

Let's build a simple component that simply counts up from 0 after it is mounted and displays the count to the user.

Here it is in React:

```
class TickTock extends React.Component {
  constructor(props) {
    super(props);

    this.state = {
      number: 0,
    };
  },
  componentDidMount() {
    this.setInterval(() => {
      this.setState({
        number: this.state.number + 1
      });
    }, 1000);
  },
  componentWillUnmount() {
    clearInterval(this.counterInterval);
  },
  render() {
    return (
      <p>{this.state.number} seconds have passed</p>
    );
  }
};
```

Here it is in Vue:

```
const TickTock = {
  template: '<p>{{ number }} seconds have passed</p>',
  data: () => ({
    number: 0,
    counterInterval: undefined,
  }),
  mounted() {
    this.counterInterval = setInterval(() => {
      this.number++;
    }, 1000);
  },
  destroyed() {
    clearInterval(this.counterInterval);
  }
};
```

With both examples, we've added some logic to clear the interval when the component is destroyed. This is to prevent memory leaks.

This brings us nicely onto our next topic: life-cycle hooks.

Life-Cycle Hooks

The way components are added and removed from the DOM are similar in both libraries, and there are methods you can add to your components in both libraries to run code at various points throughout the life cycle of a component.

Creating

A component is created and then added to the DOM. In React, you have the following four hooks:

constructor()
> Called before the component is mounted

componentWillMount()
> Called immediately before the component is mounted

render()
> Called as the component is mounted and where you return your JSX

componentDidMount()
> Called immediately after the component is mounted

In Vue, you again have four hooks, but they do slightly different things:

beforeCreate()
> Called before the component is initialized

created()
> Called after the component is initialized, but before it is added to the DOM

beforeMount()
> Called after the element is ready to be added to the DOM

mounted()
> Called after the element has been created (but not necessarily added to the DOM —use nextTick() for that)

Updating

After a component has been created and added to the DOM, the data can change, and when that happens, the component will be updated.

In React, you have the following five functions:

`componentWillReceiveProps()`
> Called before the component props are updated

`shouldComponentUpdate()`
> Called to see whether the component should be updated

`componentWillUpdate()`
> Called before the component is updated

`render()`
> Called to generate the new markup that should be returned by the component

`componentDidUpdate()`
> Called after the component is updated

In Vue, you have only two hooks:

`beforeUpdate()`
> Called when the component is about to be updated

`updated()`
> Called after the component is updated

In React, `shouldComponentUpdate()` is commonly used when using another library that manipulates the DOM, which doesn't work so well with React—it often overwrites those changes unless you tell it not to! It's also used to optimize component rendering. In Vue, this usually isn't an issue, as it works well with other libraries and handles the optimization automatically, but if you want to ensure that Vue never updates a component again, even if the data changes, you can add the `v-once` attribute to it to tell Vue to render it only once.

Setting CSS Classes

React has a commonly used library to assist when setting class attributes called *classnames*. It works like this:

```
<div className={classNames('foo', { bar: isBar })}>...</div>
```

Vue has something similar, but built in. `v-bind:class`, shortened to `:class`, doesn't just support expressions, but allows you to use objects and arrays too:

```
<div :class="['foo', { bar: isBar }]">...</div>
```

Differences

In addition to having similarities, React and Vue have differences. I won't cover all the subtle differences—the syntax differences, the method name differences—I'll just stick to the fundamentals.

Mutation

A fundamental difference between the two libraries is that with React, mutating state is heavily discouraged, whereas with Vue, replacing or mutating data is the only way to update it! We also see this with Redux and vuex—with Redux, whenever you want to change the store, you generate a new store, whereas with vuex, you mutate the existing store. We'll cover Redux and vuex later in this appendix, and for now focus on component state.

To update the state of a component in React, you use `setState`:

```
this.setState({
  user: {
    ...this.state.user,
    name: newName
  }
})
```

The new state is then merged (using a shallow merging strategy) into the state object.

With Vue, you modify the data directly:

```
this.user.name = newName;
```

This does come with caveats: for example, you have to have already defined the `name` property of the `user` object, and you can't modify array items directly, instead having to use `splice` to remove the old item and replace it with the new one. To work around this, there's a `Vue.set()` method:

```
Vue.set(this.user, 'name', newName);
```

Generally, you don't need to worry about this, but if you're running into issues with stuff not updating, this could be why. The way reactivity works in Vue and a list of the caveats can be found in "Reactivity" on page 14.

JSX Versus Templates

Another fundamental difference between React and Vue is the way you get data to display on the page. In React, famously, you use JSX, a syntax invented by Facebook to write HTML directly in JavaScript. In Vue, you can use JSX if you choose, but most people use templates instead. The templates have an Angular-like syntax, with directives and data binding.

In React, the code to generate an HTML list from an array might look like this:

```
render() {
  return (
    <ul>
      {this.state.items.map((item) => (
        <li className={classNames({ active: item.selected })}>
          {item.text}
        </li>
      ))}

      {this.state.items.length ? null : (
        <li>There are no items</li>
      )}
    </ul>
  );
}
```

There are quite a few ways that can be rewritten.

In Vue, the template looks like this:

```
<ul>
  <li v-for="item in items" :class="{ active: item.selected }">
    {{ item.text }}
  </li>
  <li v-if="!items.length">There are no items</li>
</ul>
```

I prefer the template syntax, even though I very much liked JSX when I wrote React. If you're really attached to JSX, you can use it with Vue too:

```
render(h) {
  return (
    <ul>
      {this.items.map((item) => (
        <li class={{ active: item.selected }}>
          {item.text}
        </li>
      ))}

      {this.items.length ? null : (
        <li>There are no items</li>
      )}
    </ul>
  );
}
```

Refer to Chapter 4 to see how you can set this up in your application.

CSS Modules

The final major difference is the way CSS is written in Vue. React doesn't have a built-in way to do this, but it's extremely common to use CSS modules.

In React, using CSS modules looks like this:

```
.user {
  border: 2px #ccc solid;
  background-color: white;
}

.name {
  font-size: 24px;
}

.bio {
  font-size: 16px;
  color: #333;
}
```

And the JSX:

```
import styles from './styles.css';

// ...

render() {
  return (
    <div className={styles.user}>
      <h2 className={styles.name}>{user.name}</h2>
      <p className={styles.bio}>{user.bio}</p>
    </div>
  );
}
```

Vue supports CSS modules as well, and without any plug-ins or additional build tool configuration. In Vue, it looks like this (when using single-file components):

```
<template>
  <div :class="$style.user">
    <h2 :class="$style.name">{{ user.name }}</h2>
    <p :class="$style.bio">{{ user.bio }}</p>
  </div>
</template>

<style module>
  .user { ... }
  .name { ... }
  .bio { ... }
</style>
```

More commonly, though, you'll see people using scoped CSS in Vue. Scoped CSS works by adding a random data attribute to every element output by that component, and then adding it to the end of every CSS selector. Any CSS you write in that <style> tag will apply only to the elements produced by that component.

The previous example written using scoped CSS looks like this:

```
<template>
  <div class="user">
    <h2 class="name">{{ user.name }}</h2>
    <p class="bio">{{ user.bio }}</p>
  </div>
</template>

<style scoped>
  .user { ... }
  .name { ... }
  .bio { ... }
</style>
```

The CSS in the style tag, even though we've used really generic class names that will probably apply to other elements outside the component too, will apply only to the HTML in the element. I'd still recommend using longer, more descriptive class names, though!

Scoped CSS also works well with SCSS or other CSS preprocessors, and nesting.

Ecosystem

React has a huge ecosystem because of its popularity and widespread use. Vue, as a newer and currently less popular library, doesn't have the ecosystem or community that React has yet—although it's getting better every day, and at this point, growing faster than the React ecosystem.

Unfortunately, the ecosystem for React, especially for mission-critical tasks such as routing, can often be quite fragmented. Multiple routing solutions exist for React—although react-router seems to be the most—whereas there is only one for Vue, vue-router. Although Facebook has left the community to develop nearly all of the ecosystem that isn't React itself, the people behind Vue are also the same people behind vue-router, vuex, vue-test-utils, vue-cli, and probably other official libraries in the future.

In practice, if you are using functionality that is provided by an official Vue plug-in (routing, state management, testing) you'll have a nice experience and won't have to make any choices. If you're using functionality that isn't provided by an official plug-in (internationalization, HTTP resource management) you'll probably end up having a worse experience than you would with React, which has a more established ecosystem.

For now, let's look at where the official plug-ins can help us.

Routing

We have a couple of options for handling routing in React, but by far the most widely used option is react-router. This library uses JSX to specify components that will display when the page matches a given route.

A router powered by react-router might look something like this:

```
const app = () => (
  <Router history={hashHistory}>
    <Route path="/" component={PageHome} />
    <Route path="/user/:userId" component={PageUser} />

    <Route path="/settings" component={PageSettings}>
      <Route path="/profile" component={PageSettingsProfile} />
      <Route path="/email" component={PageSettingsEmail} />
    </Route>
  </Router>
);
```

In Vue, an official library handles routing: vue-router. It doesn't use JSX, instead using an object to configure the router. The same router as the preceding one might look like this:

```
const router = new VueRouter({
  mode: 'history',
  routes: [
    {
      path: '/',
      component: PageHome
    },
    {
      path: '/user/:userId',
      component: PageUser
    },
    {
      path: '/settings',
      component: PageSettings,
      children: [
        {
          path: 'profile',
          component: PageSettingsProfile
        },
        {
          path: 'email',
          component: PageSettingsEmail
        }
      ]
    }
```

```
    ]
  });
```

Both libraries do the same things, just in different ways.

State Management

The most commonly used state management library in React is called *Redux*, and the equivalent library in Vue is the official plug-in called vuex. Both of them operate using basically the same methodology, providing a global store that you can store data in and modify throughout your app. If you're familiar with Redux, you're familiar with vuex, and vice versa; the only thing that differs between them is the terminology and the mutation differences discussed earlier.

With Redux, you have a store that contains state. You can either access the state directly, or using `react-redux` you can use the `mapStateToProps` function in the middleware to make it accessible as a prop. To update the state, you use a reducer to generate a new state. Reducers are synchronous, and to modify asynchronously, either you make the change in a component, or you can use a plug-in such as `redux-thunk` to add asynchronous actions to your app.

With vuex, you have a store that contains state. You can access the state directly, but you cannot mutate it directly: to mutate it, you use mutations, special methods within the store that are used to change the data. Mutations are synchronous only, and so to modify something asynchronously (for example, to update something from an API directly in the store), you can use actions. You can do all of that without using any additional plug-ins—just Vue and vuex.

Let's make a store that stores a list of users.

With Redux:

```
import { createStore, applyMiddleware } from 'redux';
import thunk from 'redux-thunk';

const initialState = {
  users: undefined
};

const reducer = (state = initialState, action) => {
  switch (action.type) {
    case 'SET_USERS':
      return Object.assign({}, state, {
        users: action.payload
      });

    default: return state;
  }
};
```

```
const store = createStore(reducer, applyMiddleware(thunk))
```

And in a separate actions file:

```
export function updateUsers() {
  return (dispatch, getState) => {
    return fetch('/api/users')
      .then((res) => res.json())
      .then((users) => dispatch({ type: 'SET_USERS', payload: users }));
  };
};
```

And with vuex:

```
const store = new Vuex.Store({
  state: {
    users: undefined
  },
  mutations: {
    setUsers(state, users) {
      state.users = users;
    }
  },
  actions: {
    updateUsers() {
      return fetch('/api/users')
        .then((res) => res.json())
        .then((users) => this.setUsers(users));
    }
  }
});
```

The way you use the store in components is quite different in React and in Vue.

In React, you have to wrap the entire component in the Redux middleware, which takes mapStateToProps and mapDispatchToProps arguments and passes the actions and state into the component as props.

Here's how you would update the users and get the data from the store in React:

```
import { connect } from 'react-redux';
import { updateUsers } from './actions';

class UserList extends React.Component {
  componentDidMount(state, { updateUsers }) {
    updateUsers();
  },
  render({ users }) {
    return (
      ...
    );
  }
}
```

```
const mapStateToProps = ({ users }) => users;
const mapDispatchToProps = { updateUsers };

export default connect(mapStateToProps, mapDispatchToProps)(UserList);
```

The component gets the users when it is mounted, and then when they've been loaded, they are available using just users, as the state is mapped to props thanks to the Redux middleware.

Vue and vuex are a lot easier to use together because of how nicely the ecosystem works together. You don't need to add anything special to the component; you can access the data using this.$store.

Here's the Vue equivalent of the preceding code:

```
const UserList = {
  template: '...',
  mounted() {
    this.$store.dispatch('updateUsers');
  },
  computed: {
    users() {
      return this.$store.state.users;
    }
  }
};
```

The component gets the users when it is mounted, and then when the users have been loaded, they are available using this.users.

vuex also provides helper functions to help avoid repetition in your code. For more information on vuex, check out Chapter 5.

Unit-Testing Components

A common way of unit testing React components is to use Enzyme. *Enzyme* is a library published by Airbnb that makes mounting and testing components easy.

A test in Enzyme might look like this:

```
import { expect } from 'chai';
import { shallow } from 'enzyme';
import UserView from '../components/UserView.js';

const wrapper = shallow(<UserView />);
expect(wrapper.find('p')).to.have.length(1);

const text = wrapper.find('p').text();
expect(text).to.equal('User name: Callum Macrae');
```

Vue has a similar library called vue-test-utils. Like Enzyme, it provides functionality to make mounting components, traversing the DOM, and running tests a lot easier.

Here's a similar test, but testing a Vue component using vue-test-utils instead:

```
import { expect } from 'chai';
import { shallow } from 'vue-test-utils';
import UserView from '../components/UserView.vue';

const wrapper = shallow(UserView);
expect(wrapper.contains('p')).toBe(true);

const text = wrapper.find('p').text();
expect(text).toBe('User name: Callum Macrae');
```

As you can see, they have similar syntax, so switching from one to the other shouldn't prove to be too much of a challenge.

Index

outputting to the DOM from values in Java-
Script, using Vue, 3
passing into components with slot element,
52
running through preprocessors, 74
setting dynamically, 19
HTML5 history API, 84
(see also history mode)

I

inline style binding, 71-73
array syntax, 72
providing multiple values in an array, 72
inputs and events, 30-33
inserted hook, 35
installation and setup, 3-6
interpolation
combining with directives to display text, 8
using filters with, 29
using to pass data into templates, 8

J

JavaScript
animations, 39
business logic in, 7
prerequisites for using Vue.js, viii
running through preprocessors, 74
jQuery, Vue.js vs., 1
JSX, 79-80, 145
importing components, 79
spread operator, 79
vs. templates, in React and Vue, 141

K

kebab case, 47
key, specifying with v-for, 64
keyboard events, key event modifiers, 32
keyboard modifier keys, event modifiers for, 32

L

leave transitions, 38
life-cycle hooks, 33
comparison in Vue and React, 139
in mixins and components, 60
listeners object, 126
location.pathname, 8
looping in templates, 11
(see also v-for directive)

M

mapActions function, 114, 119
mapGetters, 110, 119
mapMutations method, 112, 119
mapState helper function, 107, 119
combining with existing computed properties, 108
in modules, 117
.meta modifier key event modifier, 32
meta property (routes), 95
methods, 20
component, 44
deciding when to use, vs. data object or
computed properties, 24
differences from computed properties, 22
private methods in mixins, 61
this in, 21
mixins, 58-61
merging with components, 60
private properties in, 61
mocking and stubbing data, 126, 127
mocks, 125
modifier keys, event modifiers for, 32
modifiers (event), 31
chaining, 31
mouse event modifiers, 32
modules (CSS), in React vs. Vue, 143
modules (vuex), 116-119
file structure, 117
namespaced, 118
specifying when retrieving data from the
store, 117
mount function, 124-126
mounted hook, 33, 59, 87
mouse event modifiers, 32
mutations, 111-113
addMessages, 113
mutation helpers, 112
requirement to be synchronous, 113
triggering in namespaced modules, 119
Vue vs. React, 141

N

name attribute, adding to routes, 100
named slots, 53
namespaced modules, 118
.native modifier, 65, 94
navigation, 91-94
active class, 93

About the Author

Callum Macrae is a JavaScript developer and occasional musician based in London, UK, working at SamKnows to make the internet faster for everyone. His current favorite things to work with are Vue and SVGs (but only sometimes at the same time). He regularly contributes to open source projects including gulp and his own projects, and can be found on GitHub (*https://github.com/callumacrae*) and Twitter (*https://twitter.com/callumacrae*) (@callumacrae).

Colophon

The animal on the cover of *Vue.js: Up and Running* is the European black kite (*Milvus migrans migrans*). This diurnal raptor is found throughout central and eastern Europe, the Mediterranean, and as far west as Mongolia and Pakistan in warm months, and spends winters in sub-Saharan Africa.

The black kite is the most populous species in family Accipitridae (which includes hawks, eagles, kites, Old-World vultures, and harriers) with an estimated global population of roughly six million, due in part to its range, adaptability, and willingness to scavenge for food. The black kite is distinguished from other subspecies by the white plumage on its head, its forked tail, distinctly angled wings, and its unique call—a shrill, stuttering whinny.

Many of the animals on O'Reilly covers are endangered; all of them are important to the world. To learn more about how you can help, go to *animals.oreilly.com*.

The cover image is from *British Birds*. The cover fonts are URW Typewriter and Guardian Sans. The text font is Adobe Minion Pro; the heading font is Adobe Myriad Condensed; and the code font is Dalton Maag's Ubuntu Mono.

Learn from experts.
Find the answers you need.

Sign up for a **10-day free trial** to get **unlimited access** to all of the content on Safari, including Learning Paths, interactive tutorials, and curated playlists that draw from thousands of ebooks and training videos on a wide range of topics, including data, design, DevOps, management, business—and much more.

Start your free trial at:
oreilly.com/safari

(No credit card required.)